D1505959

The Lucent Library of Historical Eras

# A History of the Ancient Greeks

Don Nardo

LUCENT BOOKS®

THOMSON
★
TM
GALE

San Diego • Detroit • New York • San Francisco • Cleveland • New Haven, Conn. • Waterville, Maine • London • Munich

© 2004 by Lucent Books ®. Lucent Books ® is an imprint of Thomson Gale, a part of the Thomson Corporation.

Thomson is a trademark and Gale [and Lucent Books] are registered trademarks used herein under license.

*For more information, contact*
Lucent Books
27500 Drake Rd.
Farmington Hills, MI 48331-3535
Or you can visit our Internet site at http://www.gale.com

ALL RIGHTS RESERVED.
No part of this work covered by the copyright hereon may be reproduced or used in anyform or by any means—graphic, electronic, or mechanical, including photocopying, recording, taping, Web distribution or information storage retrieval systems—without the writtenpermission of the publisher.

**LIBRARY OF CONGRESS CATALOGING-IN-PUBLICATION DATA**

Nardo, Don, 1947–
    A history of the ancient Greeks / by Don Nardo.
        p. cm. — (The Lucent library of historical eras. Ancient Greece)
    Includes bibliographical references.
    ISBN 1-59018-525-0
    1. Greece—History—To 146 b.c.—Juvenile literature. I. Title.  II. Series.
DF215 .N37 2004
938—dc22

2004006322

Printed in the United States of America

# Contents

# Foreword

Looking back from the vantage point of the present, history can be viewed as a myriad of intertwining roads paved by human events. Some paths stand out—broad highways whose mileposts, even from a distance of centuries, are clear. The events that propelled the rise to power of Germany's Third Reich, its role in World War II, and its eventual demise, for example, are well defined and documented.

Other roads are less distinct, their route sometimes hidden from view. Modern legislatures may have developed from old tribal councils, for example, but the links between them are indistinct in places, open to discussion and interpretation.

The architecture of civilization—law, religion, art, science, and government—as well as the more everyday aspects of our culture—what we eat, what we wear—all developed along the historical roads and byways. In that progression can be traced every facet of modern life.

A broad look back along these roads reveals that many paths—though of vastly different character—seem to converge at a few critical junctions. These intersections are those great historical eras that echo over the long, steady course of human history, extending beyond the past and into the present.

These epic periods of time are the focus of Lucent's Library of Historical Eras. They shine through the mists of history like beacons, illuminated by a burst of creativity that propels events forward—so bright that we, from thousands of years away, can clearly see the chain of events leading to the present.

Each Lucent Library of Historical Eras consists of a set of books that highlight various aspects of these major eras. For example, the Elizabethan England library features volumes on Queen Elizabeth I and her court, Elizabethan theater, the great playwrights, and everyday life in Elizabethan London.

The mini-library approach allows for the division of each era into its most significant and most interesting parts and the exploration of those parts in depth. Also, social and cultural trends as well as illustrative documents and eyewitness accounts can be prominently featured in individual volumes.

Lucent's Library of Historical Eras presents a wealth of information to young readers. The lively narrative, fully documented primary and secondary source quotations, maps, photographs, sidebars, and annotated bibliographies serve as launching points for class discussion and further research.

In studying the great historical eras, students also develop a better understanding of our own times. What we learn from the past and how we apply it in the present may shape the future and may determine whether our era will be a guiding light to those traveling future roads.

# Introduction:
# Why Study the Greeks?

It is perfectly reasonable for a modern reader with no prior background in history to ask why it is so important for him or her to learn about the ancient Greeks. Why study what members of a civilization long dead did and said? What difference does it make to us today which peoples they defeated in battle and how these victories were achieved, what cities the Greeks founded and destroyed, how they governed themselves, the nature of the ideas and customs they spread, and where they spread them? After all, modern Greece is a small country of only moderate political and economic power and influence. Would it not make more sense for readers today to concentrate more on the history of the more powerful and influential nations that have shaped the course of recent global events—countries such as Britain, France, Germany, Russia, and the United States?

## A Vibrant, Creative Spirit

Certainly the nations mentioned above achieved notable success at various points in modern history and helped make the world what it is today. And one cannot claim to be well educated without knowing at least the main national and international leaders and events of recent times. However, if success on the world stage is accepted as a criterion for studying the history of a particular people, nation, empire, or civilization, ancient Greece has few peers or rivals. As the authors of a major recent study of Greece put it:

> The history of the ancient Greeks is one of the most improbable success stories in all of world history. A small people inhabiting a poor country on the periphery [distant edges] of the civilizations of Egypt and the Near East, the Greeks created one of the world's most remarkable cultures.[1]

Indeed, the Greeks, who were mostly poor farmers, shepherds, and traders, developed the most effective infantry (foot soldiers) in the world. These soldiers were few in number and only part-time militiamen, who in an emergency grabbed their weapons, fought a battle, and then returned home. Yet in a series of epic battles they crushed and humiliated the largest invasion force ever assembled in ancient times (sent by the king of Persia in 480 B.C.). The Greeks also founded cities and colonies from one end of the Mediterranean Sea to the other. For centuries they controlled many of the major trade routes in that sphere and spread their wares and customs throughout Europe, North Africa, and the Near East. Greek art, architecture, athletic styles, and literary forms became cultural models followed by many other ancient peoples. And finally, in less than a decade in the fourth century B.C., a Greek army led by Macedonia's young king Alexander (later called "the Great") conquered the entire Persian Empire, which stretched from Turkey to India.

The Greeks' amazing successes, touched on only briefly in these highlights of their eventful saga, would not have been possible without their unique combination of vibrancy, creative spirit, competitive drive, and at times sheer optimism. This constitutes another reason for studying the Greeks—their unique qualities as a people. "They were among the most fascinating peoples ever to live," noted historian Chester G. Starr states.

*The ancient Greeks invented the concept of political democracy. This painting depicts the Athenian democratic leader Pericles addressing a group of voters.*

One of the main values of history is that it throws light on the nature of man, his strengths and his weaknesses. From this point of view, the story of the Greeks is absorbing. They had a fresh, youthful enthusiasm and felt nothing was impossible; at the same time they gazed at life coolly and frankly and never glossed over its ills. . . . A Greek tragedy like *Oedipus the King* . . . may appear at first reading to be a lesson in reason and balanced serenity; but below the surface lurk as much murder, adultery, and ruthless passion as in any modern movie. The Greeks were one of the rare peoples in history who were never dull.[2]

## The "Bright Morning" of Western Civilization

There is an even more important reason for people today, particularly those in Western (European-based) societies, to study ancient Greece—namely, the remarkable legacy of that vanished society. Put bluntly and with no exaggeration, Western civilization was founded by the Greeks and would not exist in its present form without the momentous cultural heritage they imparted. Their architecture, sculpture, political ideas, social and military customs, literature, philosophic and scientific ideas, and language helped in profound ways to shape the cultures and ideas of all later Western lands and peoples.

These Greek influences are everywhere, though the average person rarely connects his or her origins to the Greeks. When a young man or woman goes out for the track team or watches the Olympics on television, for example, he or she is taking part in rituals that began with the establishment of the first Olympic Games in Greece in 776 B.C. Similarly, when we listen to political speeches and debates and vote to elect our leaders, we carry on a democratic tradition born in ancient Athens. And the many modern banks and government buildings fronted by rows of columns topped by triangular gables borrow and perpetuate the trademarks of classical Greek temple architecture. The theater, plays, novels, history books, gymnasiums, political bills, lawsuits, trial by jury, civil liberties, the alphabet, and many other aspects of everyday modern life were also invented by the Greeks. Even the basic intellectual approach to life and learning common today in the West is fundamentally Greek. According to popular scholar Charles Freeman:

Greek ways of exploring the cosmos, defining the problems of knowledge (and what is meant by knowledge itself), creating the language in which such problems are explored, representing the physical world and human society in the arts, [and] defining the nature of value . . . still underlie the Western cultural tradition. In some areas, the creation of mathematics, for instance, the legacy has become a universal one. All mathematicians everywhere work within a framework whose foundations are Greek.[3]

*Athletes compete in the "race in armor" in Athens. The Olympics and other ancient Greek competitions provided the basis for many modern sports.*

Thus, it is essential for the educated person to learn about the Greeks because what they did and thought long ago still affects what people do and think today. Their alliances, disputes, battles, conquests, politics, customs, beliefs, and inventions laid the groundwork for all that came later. And in a very real sense, the Greek spirit still lives on in Western society. That spirit "moves in every breath of mind that we breathe," the late, great historian Will Durant once remarked.

So much of it remains that none of us in one lifetime could absorb it all. We know its defects—its insane and pitiless wars, its stagnant slavery . . . its tragic failure to unite liberty with order and peace. But those who cherish freedom, reason, and beauty will not linger over these blemishes. They will hear behind the turmoil of political history the voices of [the great Greek democrats, artists, and thinkers]. They will be grateful for the existence of such men, and will seek their company across alien centuries. They will think of Greece as the bright morning of that Western civilization which, with all its kindred faults, is our nourishment and our life. [4]

9

# Greece in the Bronze and Dark Ages

When ancient Greece is mentioned, most people envision splendid marble temples with rows of towering columns, magnificent stone statues of perfectly formed gods and humans, and fierce warriors clad in bronze armor and wielding spears and swords. Indeed, these were integral features of Greek civilization. Yet none of the achievements associated with ancient Greece, including literature, theater, democracy, and other aspects of advanced culture, developed overnight. The so-called golden age in which the Greeks defeated Persia, constructed the mighty Parthenon temple atop Athens's central hill, and produced some of the greatest plays ever written began about 500 B.C. and lasted less than two centuries. That highly productive era was preceded by thousands of years of development by less advanced cultures in Greece.

Modern scholars are unsure of when humans first appeared in Greece. But archaeological studies show that the area was settled at least by 50,000 B.C. This was during the Paleolithic Age, or Old Stone Age, when people sustained themselves by hunting animals with weapons made of stone, wood, or bone, and gathering wild plants. Life was hard. The inhabitants, members of small tribal units, were at the mercy of the climate, which was cold much of the time since glaciers covered much of Europe; and the success of hunting depended on the numbers and movements of game, which were unpredictable.

Eventually, the glaciers receded and Greece's climate warmed up considerably. Beginning about 6500 B.C., the locals learned to grow wild grains and other plants and to domesticate animals (skills that filtered in from the more advanced cultures of the Near East). This marked the start of the Neolithic period, or New Stone Age, in Greece. The adoption of agriculture and herding was crucial to the development of civilization in the region. As noted scholar Sarah Pomeroy and her colleagues point out:

The cultivation of plants is a watershed event in the lives of a people. It allows population to increase [because the food supply is more reliable] and forces them to settle down permanently. The Neolithic Age saw the first appearance of small, permanent farming villages, made up of one-room houses . . . built of sun-dried mud bricks laid over low stone foundations, with floors of stamped earth and flat or pitched roofs made of thatch and brush. [5]

The next and by far the most important early advancement in Greece occurred about 3000 B.C. when the inhabitants learned to make tools and weapons of

## The Greeks' Indo-European Roots

*In this excerpt from their recent book about the political, social, and cultural history of ancient Greece, noted scholar Sarah B. Pomeroy and her colleagues give an excellent overview of the origins of the early Greek-speaking mainlanders.*

In the eighteenth century A.D., scholars began to recognize that ancient Greek bore many similarities to other dead languages, such as Latin, Old Persian, and Sanskrit (the language of ancient India), as well as to entire families of spoken languages, such as the Germanic and Slavic. . . . The close likenesses in vocabulary and grammatical structure among ancient languages and their descendants soon led to the insight that they had all sprung from a common linguistic ancestor, which was termed "proto-Indo-European." It was reasoned that there had once been a single Indo-European homeland, located perhaps in the vast steppes north of the Black and Caspian seas (one of several suggested homelands), and that the separate languages developed in the course of emigrations from the homeland into distant places. The speakers of proto-Greek were thus part of a great and lengthy exodus of peoples, which gradually over the centuries spread the Indo-European languages across Europe and Asia.

bronze, a mixture of the metals copper and tin. (Like agriculture, bronze smelting techniques came to Greece from the Near East.) During Greece's Bronze Age, which lasted until about 1100 B.C., people established small cities and kingdoms and began trading with neighboring regions. Eventually, these kingdoms collapsed and Greece regressed into a dark age. People forgot their heritage, and later Greeks would look back on the dimly remembered Bronze Age, Greece's first great civilized era, as the "Age of Heroes."

## Rise of the Minoans

It is not difficult to understand how the ability to smelt bronze allowed the early inhabitants of Greece to create the first advanced civilization in the region. Bronze is a far superior material for making tools and weapons than wood, stone, or copper (which was smelted before bronze). Bronze spearheads and knives, for example, are harder and keep their edges longer than stone or copper ones.

Moreover, making bronze items was more involved and time-consuming, and

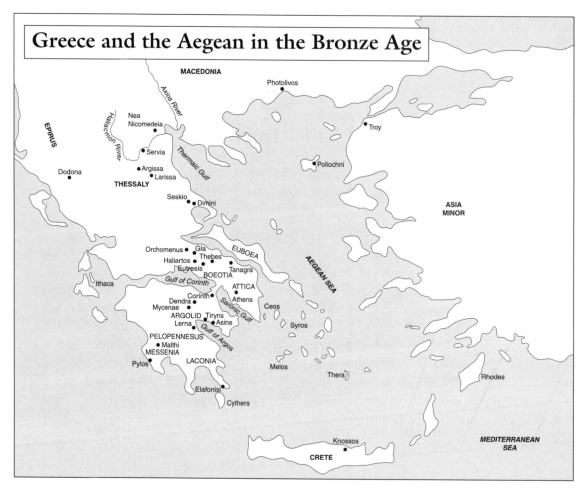

Greece and the Aegean in the Bronze Age

therefore more expensive, which made bronze more valuable. (It was also more valuable because tin was scarce and hard to find.) Lead, silver, and gold were also smelted and viewed as precious commodities. A few leading families in each region dominated production of these metals and thereby grew wealthy, which marked the rise of local aristocracies. (The word aristocrat comes from the Greek word *aristoi*, meaning "best people.") The aristocrats steadily expanded their horizons by seeking more metals, as well as other luxury items, from people living beyond the Greek sphere; in this way, trade expanded. Meanwhile, accumulated wealth allowed leading families to build large homes and exert influence and power over the common people, most of whom remained poor farmers and herders. Eventually, hereditary chiefs (those who passed their wealth and power on to their sons) and local kings emerged.

This general scenario leading to the rise of small kingdoms occurred in two separate Greek spheres during the Bronze Age. The first of these spheres was centered on the large Aegean island of Crete. About 2000 B.C., a people whom modern historians call the Minoans (after a legendary Cretan king, Minos) began building "palaces" on Crete. It appears that these were more than just residences for local royal families. The palaces likely also served various communal, administrative, religious, and ceremonial purposes.

In time, these structures became immense, multistoried, and richly decorated. The largest of all, located at Knossos, near Crete's northern coast, was excavated in the early twentieth century by English archae-

*The stone throne in the "Palace of Minos" at Knossos, backed by a fresco depicting legendary beasts called griffins.*

ologist Arthur Evans. He found magnificent frescoes (paintings done on wet plaster), a throne room with the throne still intact, and the remains of sophisticated plumbing facilities that provided running water and efficient waste removal. Regarding the latter, classical scholar J.V. Luce writes:

The excellence and "modernity" of the plumbing and drainage system of the palace of Minos has always excited admiring comment. The queen's [suite] had its own separate bathroom and toilet. On the northeast corner of the palace, an elaborate series of runnels [water channels] . . . carried the run-off of rain water through two small settling tanks to a large cistern [water storage container].[6]

Evans and other scholars also deduced that the Minoan economy was collective in nature and reflected the wide differences in social classes that had evolved during the Bronze Age. In this system, the central administration was based in the palace and headed by the king and his leading nobles. They controlled and exploited the farmers and craftsmen who produced essential goods. Scholar Thomas R. Martin explains it this way:

> The central authority told producers how much they had to contribute to the central collection facility and also decided what each member of the society would receive for subsistence and reward. . . . Scribes meticulously recorded what came in and what went out by writing on clay tablets kept in the palace. This process of economic redistribution applied to craft specialists as well as food producers. . . . Overseas trade probably operated as a monopoly through the palace system, too, with little role for independent merchants and traders.[7]

Evans found that the scribes recorded the flow of goods using two separate writing systems. He called one script "Linear A" and the other "Linear B." Unable to decipher either, he and other scholars of his day assumed they were both written forms of long-dead non-Greek languages.

## The Mainland Mycenaeans

It turned out that this assumption was only half right. The Minoans, who expanded their influence to nearby Aegean islands, creating a sort of mini–maritime empire, did speak a non-Greek tongue. However, there were Greek speakers in the region, too. It appears that the Minoans came to exert strong cultural and perhaps political influence over these early Greeks, who occupied the second sphere of small kingdoms in Bronze Age Greece, located on the mainland. Historians call the mainlanders Mycenaeans. The name comes from the massive stone palace-citadel of Mycenae, situated on a rocky hilltop in the northeastern Peloponnesus (the large peninsula that makes up the southern third of Greece).

It is uncertain when the first Mycenaeans arrived in Greece. Scholarly estimates range from 2100 B.C. to 1600 B.C., but the consensus is that they came from the north and northeast in two or more waves beginning about 2000 B.C. At first, they were culturally backward in comparison with the Minoans, whose society they seem to have envied and in many ways copied. The Mycenaean economic system, for instance, appears to have had a similar pyramid-like form. "At its base," historians Carol G. Thomas and Craig Conant remark,

> the great majority of the population labored in their small fields to produce a surplus, which was gathered for collective storage within the protected citadel. Between the base and apex [of the pyramid] was a smaller though still sizable group of craftsmen and merchants, much of whose labor [was] monopolized by the palace in return for

# Mycenae Erected by Cyclopes?

*The following description of the massive citadel at Mycenae by scholars Carol G. Thomas and Craig Conant (from their book* Citadel to City-State*) emphasizes its imposing location and the size of its defensive walls.*

The ancient citadel of Mycenae is situated on a rocky, roughly triangular hill. . . . Even without fortifications, the hill is highly defensible. To the north the land drops away precipitously, and while the south slope is gentler, it is by no means easy. . . . Natural defensibility was enhanced by human technology. In the Late Bronze Age, walls some 900 meters [nearly 3,000 feet] in length ringed the entire crest of the hill, enclosing an area of more than 38,000 square meters [9.4 acres]. Because the wall consisted largely of enormous rough-hewn blocks and unhewn boulders reaching a width of eight meters [twenty-six feet] in places, Greeks of a later age referred to such walls as Cyclopean and told the tale of how Perseus, the legendary founder of Mycenae, employed giant Cyclopes [one-eyed monsters] . . . to construct the walls.

*A nineteenth-century engraving reconstructs the original appearance of the citadel at Mycenae based on existing ruins.*

rations produced by the peasants. At the top of the pyramid were the administrative and military elites and the central manager, named in the palace records as the *wanax*. . . . The *wanax* and his peers provided security against famine and protection against enemies for those situated lower on the pyramid. [8]

The Mycenaeans also borrowed styles of dress, artistic motifs, and other cultural aspects from the Minoans.

The two peoples did have considerable differences, however. First and foremost was the fact that they spoke different languages. In the 1950s, a brilliant young British scholar named Michael Ventris deciphered the Linear B script, which had been found on both the mainland and the islands. He proved that it was an early form of Greek. (Linear A, which is still largely undeciphered, seems to have been a written form of the non-Greek Minoan language.) The Mycenaeans also worshipped a strong male deity, Zeus (whom they brought with them from their original homeland to the northeast), and they built religious sanctuaries to this and other gods inside their palace-citadels. In contrast, the principal Minoan deity was a mother goddess, and shrines to her and other gods were often located in caves and on mountaintops.

## War and Natural Disasters Devastate Crete

Whatever the similarities and differences between the Minoans and Mycenaeans, the latter established small kingdoms, each dom-

*This vase painting from ca. 570 B.C. shows the hero Theseus and his men at a wedding party. Theseus may have been a real Mycenaean king.*

inated by a stone palace-citadel, across southern Greece. Among others, these included Tiryns, situated not far south of Mycenae; Pylos on the southwestern coast of the Peloponnesus; Athens in Attica, a large peninsula of eastern Greece; and Thebes, Orchomenus, and Gla in Boeotia (bee-OH-shya), the region just north of Attica. The Minoans, who had a powerful fleet of ships, may have politically or even militarily dominated some of these mainland kingdoms for some undetermined length of time. The Mycenaeans steadily grew stronger, however, and began to assert themselves beyond the confines of the mainland. Sometime during the 1400s B.C., the forces of one or more of the Mycenacean kingdoms invaded Crete and took over Knossos and the other Minoan palaces.

This general series of events may be the basis for the well-known Greek myth of the Athenian hero-king Theseus. According to the story, each year the king of Knossos demanded and received from Athens a ransom consisting of fourteen young men and women. The captives were fed to the Minotaur, a creature who was half-man and half-bull. (This creature was probably a garbled memory of Minoan priests; some evidence suggests that they wore bull masks when performing sacrifices.) Theseus eventually ended this humiliation by leading a military expedition against Crete. According to the first-century A.D. Greek biographer Plutarch, "When the ships were ready, he set out" and, on reaching northern Crete, he "was able to seize the harbor, disembark his men, and reach Knossos before his arrival was discov-

ered." Theseus and his men "fought a battle," after which he slew the Minotaur. After that, the Cretans "swore that they would never in the future begin a war with Athens."[9] Perhaps this episode, if it is actually based on real events, marked the beginning of a series of invasions that finally brought the Mycenaeans to power in Crete.

Scholars do not know for sure why the Minoans, who had long been so prosperous and powerful, were unable to fend off the mainlanders. But the answer may lie on the small island of Thera (today called Santorini), located about eighty miles north of Crete. In about 1600 B.C., the volcano on Thera erupted with unprecedented violence in what some scientists have called the most destructive natural disaster in recorded history. Earthquakes and airborne blast waves toppled many buildings on Crete. Meanwhile, towering sea waves drowned untold thousands of Minoans and wrecked many of their ships and docks. "In addition to the effects of the blast and tidal waves," says Luce,

the hills and valleys of eastern Crete were covered to a considerable depth of ash fall-out. . . . We can envisage that the Minoans of central and eastern Crete who escaped the waves may well have found much of their land uncultivable, their orchards destroyed . . . and their buildings flattened. This factor of fall-out could be the explanation for . . . the westward migration [of the Minoan population] which is clear from the archaeological evidence.[10]

17

*The volcano beneath Thera's central bay (created when the island's central portion collapsed in ca. 1600 B.C.) erupts in this nineteenth-century painting.*

This may well explain why Minoan civilization went into a fatal decline. Not only were large numbers of lives lost and farmland ruined, but most of the Minoans' ships, the mainstay of their empire, were also destroyed. There is no doubt that the Minoans did survive the catastrophe. They rebuilt many of their damaged buildings and must have built more ships and partially replenished their population. But they were unable to make a total recovery before the Mycenaean warlords swept down from mainland Greece and overran them in the fifteenth century B.C.

## Sudden and Tremendous Upheaval

After taking over Crete, the Mycenaeans dominated the Aegean seaways for the next two centuries. In addition to engaging in regular trade, they raided the coasts of Asia Minor (what is now Turkey). Toward the end of this period, an alliance of Mycenaean kings may have sacked the prosperous city of Troy, on Asia Minor's northwestern coast. The legendary eighth-century B.C. Greek bard Homer told about such an event in his epic poem the *Iliad*. And evidence uncovered in Troy's ruins indicates that the city did undergo a siege about 1220 B.C., the approximate period in which the mythical Trojan War supposedly took place. It remains unproven that this was the siege described by Homer or, for that matter, that the war in the *Iliad* ever actually took place. But most of the myths recorded by later Greek writers derived from the Age of Heroes, which correlates with the late Bronze Age, when the Mycenaeans were at their height. And it is likely that distorted memories of some of their deeds were handed down as legends to later generations of Greeks.

Separating the Mycenaeans from those later Greeks was the relatively sudden and catastrophic collapse of the Bronze Age kingdoms and their way of life. About 1200 B.C. or shortly thereafter, the Aegean sphere, as well as many parts of the Near East, underwent a period of tremendous upheaval. Most of the major Mycenaean strongholds were sacked and burned, never to be rebuilt. Historians have proposed a number of theories to explain this turmoil, including civil conflicts and a disruption of farming and trade leading to the ruin of the palace economies. Martin summarizes a more recent explanation, suggested by Vanderbilt University scholar Robert Drews:

> Previously, the preponderance of military might [in the Mycenaean kingdoms] had lain with . . . chariots carrying archers. . . . These chariot forces had been supplemented by infantrymen, mostly foreign mercenaries. . . . These hired foot soldiers [eventually] realized that they could use their long swords and javelins [throwing spears] to defeat the chariot forces in direct battle by swarming in a mass against their vehicle-mounted overlords. Emboldened . . . and motivated by a lust for booty, the motley bands of mercenaries attacked [the palaces and towns]. . . . With no firm organization

among themselves, the rebels fatally weakened the civilizations they betrayed . . . but were incapable of or disinterested in putting any new political systems into place.[11]

Perhaps the collapse of the Bronze Age centers was the result of all of these causes combined. In other words, maybe the Mycenaeans fought one another until all were weak enough to allow bands of foreign troops to swoop in; destroy their chariots, palaces, and farms; and kill their leaders and scribes.

Whatever the cause or causes of the disaster, Greek civilization suddenly declined and entered a cultural dark age. No longer

*This painting shows Greek warriors leaving their hiding place in the wooden horse in order to sack Troy.*

inhabited and kept up, the citadels at Mycenae, Tiryns, and other mainland sites began to decay, while literacy, record keeping, artistic skills, and other elements that had supported Bronze Age society were lost. Besides the ruined palaces, all that remained were memories of the powerful individuals who had lived in them. These memories became increasingly dim and exaggerated over time until they were transformed into colorful, romantic legends of a time when heroes, monsters, and gods roamed the land.

## A Sort of Sleep

The Dark Age of Greece lasted approximately three centuries. It must be emphasized that one reason why scholars label it "dark" is that no writings and little archaeological evidence have survived from that era. So next to nothing is known about the history and lives of its people. The other reason the period was dark is that, overall, civilization declined from the levels it had attained in Minoan-Mycenaean times. Society experienced major decreases in population (for at least the first century or so), for example. There was also widespread poverty and a deterioration of both the standard of living and cultural standards. In general, large-scale farming, which had been a mainstay of local Mycenaean economies, was abandoned in favor of hunting and raising animals, activities more easily accomplished by small, impoverished

### A Greek Historian Remembers the Dark Age

*In his chronicle of the Peloponnesian War (Rex Warner's translation), the great fifth-century B.C. Greek historian Thucydides included this brief description of early Greece, likely based on surviving folklore. Modern scholars believe that, except for overemphasizing the role played by foreign intruders, it captures conditions in the Dark Age fairly accurately.*

The country now called Greece had no settled population in ancient times; instead there was a series of migrations, as the various tribes, being under the constant pressure of invaders who were stronger than they were, were always prepared to abandon their own territory. There was no commerce, and no safe communication either by land or sea; the use they made of their land was limited to the production of necessities; they had no surplus left over . . . and no regular system of agriculture, since they lacked the protection of fortifications and at any moment an invader might appear and take their land away from them. Thus . . . they showed no reluctance in moving from their homes, and therefore built no cities of any size or strength, nor acquired any important resources.

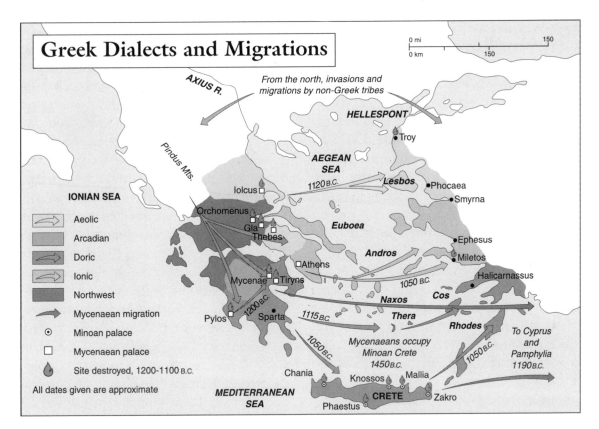

## Greek Dialects and Migrations

0 mi 150
0 km 150

From the north, invasions and migrations by non-Greek tribes

AXIUS R.

HELLESPONT

Pindus Mts.

Troy

AEGEAN SEA

IONIAN SEA

Iolcus

1120 B.C.

Lesbos

Phocaea

Smyrna

Orchomenus

Euboea

Gla

Thebes

Ephesus

Andros

Miletos

Athens

Halicarnassus

Mycenae

Tiryns

1050 B.C.

Naxos

Cos

Pylos

1200 B.C.

Sparta

1115 B.C.

Thera

Rhodes

To Cyprus and Pamphylia 1190 B.C.

1050 B.C.

Mycenaeans occupy Minoan Crete 1450 B.C.

Chania

Knossos

Mallia

1050 B.C.

CRETE

Zakro

MEDITERRANEAN SEA

Phaestus

**Legend:**
- Aeolic
- Arcadian
- Doric
- Ionic
- Northwest
- Mycenaean migration
- ⊙ Minoan palace
- ☐ Mycenaean palace
- Site destroyed, 1200-1100 B.C.

All dates given are approximate

groups of people. Citing evidence found at Nichoria, a tiny Dark Age village located near the deserted palace-center at Pylos, Thomas and Conant point out:

Animals played a great role in sustaining the lives of the inhabitants. . . . Analysis of cattle bones suggests that the proportion of beef in the diet at Nichoria [which had been] about 11% at the end of the Bronze Age . . . rose steadily to 45% in [the] Dark Age. . . . [Also] more dogs lived in the small community. Bones of the red deer, and later the roe deer, are proportionally greater in Dark Age Nichoria than they

were during the Mycenaean age. These finds combine to suggest that [the] settlers . . . spent a good bit of time pasturing domesticated animals . . . and hunting wild animals in lands that, with less intensive cultivation, were reverting to woodlands. Dogs would be invaluable aides to humans in both occupations, especially since human numbers were so few. In fact, pasturage and hunting require less labor than farming.[12]

Nevertheless, a few crops were grown on a small scale, including wheat, grapes, cherries, and olives. Olive trees are particularly long-lived and were likely a fortunate inheritance from Mycenaean times.

Although some small villages like Nichoria remained more or less stable, the Dark Age was also marked by frequent and sometimes large-scale migrations of local populations. Some people left the mainland, crossed the Aegean, and settled on the western coasts of Asia Minor, an area that later came to be called Greek Ionia. Other mainlanders abandoned their towns and villages and moved to other areas of the mainland. Some of these population movements may have been the result of disruptions caused by widespread death and destruction during the collapse of Mycenaean culture. However, at least some of those who migrated were displaced by immigrants who entered Greece from the north in the first century of the Dark Age. (Scholars call these immigrants, who also spoke Greek, the Dorians.)

Evidence suggests that many of the displaced mainlanders took refuge in small pockets of Mycenaean society that had survived the recent upheavals. The most notable of these areas was Athens, in Attica, which appears to have somehow escaped the brunt of the turmoil. Nevertheless, within a few generations the inhabitants, like other Greeks, lost their Mycenaean identity and most of their heritage and began to build a new culture.

Meanwhile, a few smaller Mycenaean sites seem to have survived well into the Dark Age. One that has attracted the attention of scholars since the early 1980s is Lefkandi, in the western part of Euboea (the large island lying along the eastern coast of the Greek mainland). There, archaeologists found the remains of the largest Dark Age building yet uncovered. Dating to roughly 1000 B.C., it originally measured about 146 by 30 feet and had a high roof supported by wooden pillars. Its owner was apparently a chief or warlord of considerable wealth and distinction. Beside his cremated remains the excavators found a magnificent iron sword and spearhead and the skeletons of four horses, probably his chariot team.

The fine house and goods of the individual whom modern scholars have come to call the "Hero of Lefkandi" were clearly exceptional for Dark Age Greece. Yet his iron sword and spearhead demonstrate that, despite widespread poverty and cultural decline, Greece was neither primitive nor stagnant during that era. As had occurred in prior millennia, new ideas and skills began to filter in from the Near East. The most important of these was iron smelting, which spread across Greece between about 1050 and 950 B.C. This was a major technological advance, since iron tools and weapons are much tougher and more durable than bronze ones. Other equally momentous advances would soon follow. Having drifted for awhile in a sort of cultural sleep, the Greeks were about to reawaken and begin to fashion a civilization like none the world had seen before.

Chapter

# 2

# The Rise of City-States and Greece's Rebirth

S tarting about 800 B.C., Greece rapidly began to emerge from its Dark Age into the light of a new era of economic prosperity and political and cultural rebirth. Modern scholars call that era, which lasted roughly three centuries, the Archaic Age. Greece's population, which had begun to rise again in the late Dark Age, burgeoned in early Archaic times, and this spurred the foundation of many new towns. Some of these were in mainland Greece and the nearby islands; others appeared along the lengthy coasts of the Mediterranean and Black seas. At the same time, trade with ports in those seas underwent tremendous expansion. This infused Greece with large quantities of goods, both utilitarian and luxury items.

Population expansion and other factors also influenced a rebirth of agriculture across Greece. Raising livestock remained important but became secondary to the intensive cultivation of olives and vines. Even more important, the new farmers were not poor peasants trapped in a collective system controlled by a few nobles, as in Mycenaean times. Archaic Greece witnessed the rise of a whole new class of independent farmers who owned and worked their own plots. These hardy, self-reliant individuals were destined to transform not only the land but also the political, social, and military institutions of their communities. Noted scholar Victor D. Hanson remarks:

# Greek Farming Methods

*In his widely read book* The Ancient Greeks, *the late classical scholar Chester G. Starr provided this useful brief description of the farming methods that emerged in Greece during the Archaic Age and continued for many centuries.*

Nearly all Greeks spent their years from childhood to old age in the annual round of agricultural work. Since crops were weeded and harvested by hand, a farmer and his family could scarcely cultivate more than 2 or 3 acres in any one season; and the absence of modern fertilizers forced him to leave part of his land uncultivated each year so that it could regain its fertility. . . . The farmer broke the soil in a spring or summer plowing, and he plowed a second, final time in the fall. Greek plows were simple wooden tools, the bottom of which was possibly tipped with iron, pulled by oxen, and they did little more than break the thin soils. Behind the plow, a member of the farmer's family or a slave . . . [tossed out the seeds]. In May, everyone who could work labored from dawn to dark to cut the ripe grain with sickles. . . . Grain was threshed on stone threshing floors by oxen . . . to separate the wheat from the chaff. . . . In addition to wheat and barley on the flat lands, farmers cultivated on the hillsides olive trees and vines, which could live during the dry summer because they had roots that grew deep enough to reach moist ground.

No ingredient . . . is so dramatically successful in agriculture as free will, the ability to implement a new idea, to develop a proven routine, to learn . . . from the hard taskmaster of error, to be left *alone* from government planning to grope for a plan of survival. Self-initiative, once turned loose on the soil, can result in spectacular results for both the farmer and the surrounding community. . . . [In such a situation] a transformation in both values and ideology ensues.[13]

A major part of that transformation took the form of political growth and experimentation. Greece's many isolated communities, which had developed separate, individual identities during the Dark Age, emerged as full-blown city-states in the eighth century B.C. The Greeks called the city-state the polis (plural is poleis). The average polis consisted of a town (when possible built around a central hill called an acropolis) surrounded by small supporting villages and plots of farmland. These city-states developed differing local governments and traditions and came to think of themselves as tiny separate nations. (In fact, Greece was never a united country in ancient times.) It was from this burst of political experimentation that democracy first emerged near the end of the Archaic Age.

An important element of the new political and social dynamic of the emerging city-states was a strong competitive spirit. It was characterized by a desire to acquire honor and respect and to be not only better but the best in a given situation or field of endeavor. This spirit increasingly came to characterize not only rivalries among individuals within a community but also rivalries among the city-states themselves. Sometimes this competitive spirit expressed itself peacefully, through friendly athletic competitions; accordingly, this was the age in which the Olympic Games were born. Other times the competitive spirit was manifested in warfare among the poleis, and to that end, the Greeks developed a new and deadly mode of fighting, one that would eventually help them achieve dominance over peoples living far beyond Greece's borders.

## "The Dancing Floor of War"

The new style of warfare developed by the Greeks was built around and largely conducted by the class of small independent farmers who were creating a revolution in agriculture. Indeed, these tough, independent men became more than the economic backbone of the community. They quickly learned a central fact of free land ownership. Namely, their plots, which were vital to sustaining their lives and the life of their polis, needed to be secure from outside threats.

At first, the most common aggressors were farmers from neighboring poleis who sought to expand their own territories. To protect themselves, therefore, the men in each city-state organized a local citizen militia. The members, mostly farmers, but sometimes also artisans and merchants who worked in the town center, took up arms in an emergency and then returned to their jobs when the emergency was over.

By the seventh century B.C., these militiamen had developed their own style of fighting. Extremely effective both defensively and offensively, it was built around heavily armored infantry soldiers called hoplites. The term hoplite probably derives from the Greek word *hopla*, meaning "heavy equipment." This equipment consisted of bronze body armor (helmet, chest protector, and lower-leg protectors called greaves), a bronze shield, a thrusting spear with an iron tip, and a short iron-bladed slashing sword. Because of this weighty ensemble, hoplites came to be called "heavy infantry," thereafter a common term in Western warfare.

The hoplites fought in a special battlefield formation called a phalanx. A phalanx was essentially a long block of soldiers several ranks (lines) deep. A depth of eight ranks was most common, but sometimes, to meet the needs of a particular situation, commanders called for more than eight or as few as three or four ranks.

The soldiers in these ranks worked in unison on the battlefield. Their uplifted shields created an unbroken protective barrier that was very difficult to penetrate. And when the phalanx began to move, it possessed a tremendous and lethal forward momentum. As the formation made contact with the enemy lines, the hoplites in the front rank jabbed their spears at their opponents. Meanwhile, those in the rear ranks pushed at their comrades' backs, pressing them forward at the enemy. This explains why the second-century B.C. Greek historian Polybius said, "So long as the phalanx retains its characteristic form and strength, nothing can withstand its charge or resist it face to face."[14]

The accepted procedures of Greek phalanx fighting were highly ritualistic and formal. One

*Members of a phalanx march toward the enemy in open order. Before attacking, they will close ranks.*

side duly notified the other of impending battle, after which the two phalanxes faced each other on a predetermined, flat stretch of ground. Several small plains bordering major city-states were used repeatedly; one witnessed so many battles over the centuries that it became known as the "dancing floor of war." Like duelists settling a matter of honor, the formations marched directly at each other, collided, and shoved each other back and forth until one side

**The Phalanx**

**Open Phalanx**
5–6 feet
between
soldiers

**Closed Phalanx**
When maneuvering into battle, the rear half of each file moves forward to create a "shield wall."

*The Greek phalanx was particularly devastating when used against non-Greeks, whose less organized infantry and cavalry were mowed down by Greek spears.*

gave way. The side that withdrew was the loser and lost face, while the winner gained in prestige.

Though this formal approach to warfare at first appeared strange to non-Greeks, it had an underlying logic. The fighting was quick and decisive, usually produced minimal serious casualties, and almost always spared civilians and towns. This allowed communities to defend their territory and honor through combat, while avoiding long, devastating wars.

## From Oligarchy to Democracy

At the same time that independent Greek farmer-fighters were beginning to gain power in the emerging city-states, those states were engaged in vigorous and fertile bursts of political experimentation. The structure and institutions of these local governments varied considerably. Yet they had one important similarity: an increasingly strong emphasis on the needs, rights, participation, and eventually political voices of the citizenry. As Charles Freeman puts it:

> The ancient Greeks could never conceive of a polis independently of its citizens . . . and the emergence of its comparatively sophisticated political structure . . . probably lies in the emergence of a peasant class of farmers as

# A Hoplite's Distinctive Shield

A hoplite's shield, called a *hoplon* or *aspis,* was about three feet in diameter and weighed roughly eighteen pounds. It curved inward, making it slightly concave, and had a wooden core reinforced on the outside by a coating of bronze. On the inside, it was lined with leather and had a logical and effective gripping arrangement. The soldier passed his left forearm through a bronze strip with a loop in the middle and grasped a leather handle on the shield's rim with his left hand. Thus, the shield rested on his arm, which allowed him to let go of the handle and hold a spare weapon in his left hand. This ingenious system also helped to relieve the burden of the shield's considerable weight.

The outer surfaces of such shields featured decorations called shield "devices," some of them the faces of mythical monsters intended to strike fear in the enemy. Other shield devices denoted family background or military rank. And still others indicated which city-state the hoplite hailed from. For example, Spartan soldiers painted the letter L on their shields (standing for Lacedaemon, the traditional ancient name for Sparta). Similarly, the shields of Athenian hoplites eventually bore the letter A.

*The hoplite at left is in attack mode, while the other stands at ease before battle.*

arable farming takes root. What do such farmers require? Security is one need and this presupposes some form of community organization so that all can join in the protection of their land, and the stores of surplus food they accumulate, against rival communities. . . . Here is the potential for political structures based on the involvement of citizens in their own government, at least through participation in an assembly in a local center.[15]

The development of an empowered citizenry in Greece was a slow and uneven process that proceeded in stages in Archaic times and beyond. In the first stage in most places, power passed from the hands of Dark Age chieftains to ruling councils composed of several community leaders, who at first were all aristocrats. This form of government is known as an oligarchy, from a Greek word meaning "rule of the few." Some city-states held on to their oligarchic councils for hundreds of years.

In contrast, the common people in a number of other poleis steadily grew hostile to aristocratic rule, which allowed ambitious leaders to experiment with new forms of government. One form was known as tyranny. For a fairly brief period that began in the mid-600s B.C., men in several leading city-states gained power by enlisting the support of citizens who wanted to reduce the authority of the aristocrats. At first, most of these so-called tyrants upheld local laws, supported the arts, and enjoyed wide popular support. In time, however, some became more oppressive or brutal, giving the word tyrant the negative connotation it has today. Whether they were good or bad rulers, the tyrants did not last long in Greece. To remain in power, a tyrant required popular support, especially from his community's soldiers. But the citizens of many poleis, including the soldiers, increasingly demanded a bigger voice in government for themselves, which inevitably led them to oust the tyrants.

This movement toward more democratic ideals occurred at different rates in different places. It gained the most steam in Athens, which by 600 B.C. had become one of the largest and most populous of the city-states. Like many other Greek states in the Archaic Age, Athens was ruled first by a council of aristocrats (aided by three and later nine civic administrators called archons). The city also had a citizen assembly that met from time to time. But that body had no real say in government, which remained in the hands of a few nobles. By the early sixth century B.C., the aristocrats and common people were so at odds with

*This engraving shows the Athenian lawgiver Solon dictating his laws to a group of scribes.*

each other that civil war seemed imminent. Seeking to avoid bloodshed, in 594 B.C. the two sides asked a respected citizen named Solon to work out a compromise. He created a fairer system of laws, increased the status of the assembly, allowed people of all social classes to serve as jurors in trials, and made it easier for commoners to get out of debt and achieve higher social standing.

Despite these social and legal reforms, disagreements between the commoners and aristocrats in Athens continued to flare up. In 546 B.C. an ambitious man named Pisistratus took advantage of the unstable situation and became tyrant. After he died, his son, Hippias, took his place. A strong aristocratic faction eventually managed to get rid of Hippias. Seeing that these nobles wanted only to gain power for themselves, the leader of a rival aristocratic faction, Cleisthenes, wisely appealed to the commoners for help. After eliminating his enemies, in 508 B.C. Cleisthenes played the leading role in the creation of a full-fledged democracy, the world's first, in which the citizen assembly held the lion's share of power. This series of events laid the groundwork for Athens's subsequent rise to political and cultural greatness.

# Economic Renewal and the Heroic Revival

During the same years when Athens and other city-states were experimenting with various political systems, Greece was growing increasingly prosperous and steadily rising from its formerly backward state. Trade was the major stimulus to economic renewal. Whereas in the Dark Age few Greeks ever ventured far from their home valleys or islands, in Archaic times Greek ships ranged across the known world. A good deal of the trade was with port cities recently founded by the Phoenicians, an adventurous maritime trading people whose home bases were located along the coasts of Palestine. Greek traders also established trading posts of their own in Syria, Italy, and eventually North Africa and elsewhere. Many of these posts grew into thriving city-states that traded with the poleis in the Aegean sphere.

Metal ores, foods, fabrics, and other material goods were not the only valuable imports Greece received from these overseas contacts. From the Phoenicians the Greeks also borrowed a simple alphabet. This made it possible for the Greeks to become literate again and to produce literature themselves. During the Dark Age, news of major events and tales of heroes and gods of past ages had been passed along orally by storytellers called bards. Bards roamed from town to town and recited their verses in exchange for food and lodging or a small fee.

The most popular of all these stories were Homer's epic poems—the more-than-fifteen-thousand-line *Iliad* and the twelve-thousand-line *Odyssey* (which tells about the later adventures of one of the Greek kings who besieged Troy). Sometime during the Archaic Age (exactly when is still disputed) these works were committed to paper. Thereafter, every Greek became intimately familiar with them, and they exerted a profound influence on

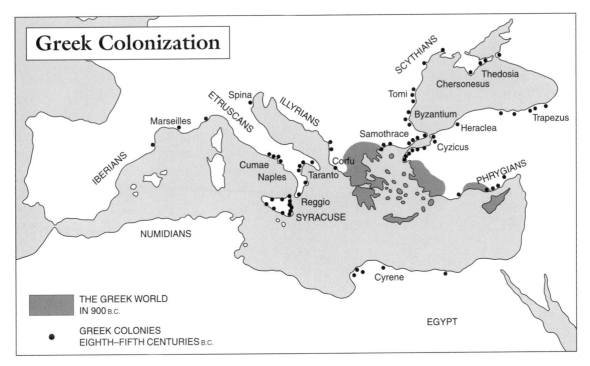

Greek culture and thought. Homer's detailed descriptions of the gods helped to shape the way people viewed these deities. The Homeric epics also became the primary literary texts studied by Greek schoolchildren. In addition, these works served as a culturally unifying force. Among the disunited city-states, who often squabbled, the epics were seen as the common property of all Greeks and a reminder that they once stood together against a common enemy.

The fascination with and admiration for the heroes of Homer's epics was part of what scholars often refer to as the heroic revival, which spread through the Greek lands in the early Archaic Age. By this time, the major events and figures of the Bronze Age had crystallized into popular myths about heroes of the dim past. And people now started to recognize the totality of these stories as a cultural heritage to be proud of and perpetuate. "Greeks everywhere began to express their connection to the heroic past in new and dramatic ways," Sarah Pomeroy and her colleagues explain.

Numerous ancient tombs (mostly Mycenaean) that had been ignored throughout the Dark Age began to receive . . . offerings [sacrificial gifts], an indication that their anonymous inhabitants were now worshiped as "heroes." Other kinds of hero cults [were celebrated] . . . at shrines set up in honor of legendary heroic figures. . . . The impetus behind hero cults was the belief that the great men and women of the Heroic Age had power in death to protect and help the people. . . . Wealthy Greeks of the later eighth century also expressed an urge to connect with the past through heroic-style burials . . . [like those described] in epic poetry. [16]

# The Glory of Sport

The heroic revival, especially the widespread reverence for Homer's epics, was in a sense Panhellenic; that is, it involved and affected all Greeks rather than the inhabitants of only one or a few local city-states. (The term Panhellenism comes from the root words Hellenes, the name the Greeks called themselves, and pan, meaning "all.") Indeed, despite the political disunity and frequent disagreements among the city-states, Panhellenism became a potent force in the Archaic Age because all Greeks recognized that they shared the same language, culture, and religion.

One of the most important Panhellenic activities that developed in Archaic times consisted of athletic games attended by all Greeks. The most famous and popular of these competitions was the Olympic Games, which began, according to tradition, in 776 B.C. The Olympic festival, which honored Zeus, leader of the gods, was held at Olympia, in southwestern Greece, every four years. (Three other athletic festivals were nearly as important—the Pythian Games, held at Delphi, in central Greece; the Isthmian Games, staged in Corinth, in the northern Peloponnesus; and the Nemean Games, held at Nemea, a few miles south of Corinth. In addition, every polis held its own local games, of which those staged in Athens became the most prestigious.)

The importance and sanctity of the Olympic Games to all Greeks was demonstrated by the Olympic truce. In the months leading up to the great event, three special heralds visited every Greek state. They not only invited all to attend the games, but also announced the truce, eventually lasting three months, during which all participating states were forbidden to make war. The truce ensured safe passage for the thousands of competitors, spectators, and religious pilgrims who attended the games. Violations were rare and resulted in exclusion from the games and/or heavy fines.

The Olympics and other major games were also important, both in Archaic times and for many centuries afterward, as an outlet for the Greeks' intense competitive spirit and desire to achieve honor and prestige. Contrary to a common modern myth, love of sport was not the only reason they competed. Winning athletes always received numerous financial and other awards when they returned to their home cities, including valuable goods and cash. Moreover, a number of poleis awarded victorious native sons with free meals for life. And the most successful athletes became the objects of heroic songs and statues.

# A Deeply Religious Spirit

Another Panhellenic activity that profoundly shaped the emerging city-states in Archaic times was religious worship, which permeated Greek culture at all levels. In Chester Starr's words, "Into all aspects of life the

Greeks interwove a deeply religious spirit to a degree which most of us today would find hard to understand."[17] Indeed, religious faith was so pervasive that prayers or other rituals accompanied all meals, public meetings, athletic events, theatrical presentations, births, marriages, funerals, journeys and voyages, and even battles. As a result, as the city-states coalesced in Archaic Greece, their inhabitants came to see religion as a public, community-wide concern. It was believed that the goodwill of the gods could not be maintained unless everyone was pious; if one citizen showed disrespect for the gods, the whole community might suffer some form of divine wrath.

This need to revere and respect the gods was especially crucial in the case of a city's patron deity. The Greeks believed that certain gods favored certain cities above others, so in addition to recognizing all the gods, each city had a personal patron god who was thought to watch over and protect the community. Athena, goddess of war and wisdom, was Athens's patron, while the patron god of Corinth was Poseidon, ruler of the seas. In addition to the chief god Zeus, other major deities included Hera, Zeus's wife and protector of women; Dionysus, who kept the earth fertile; and Apollo, god of prophecy and healing. These and several other gods were known as the "Olympians" because early traditions claimed they dwelled atop Mt. Olympus (in the northern region of Thessaly), the tallest mountain in Greece.

The Greeks performed public sacrifices of animals and plants at altars set up next to temples erected to these deities. (No worship took place inside a temple to respect a god's privacy, as he or she was believed to inhabit the structure from time to time.) In the early Archaic period temples were built of wood. But beginning in the early 600s B.C., there

*This drawing purports to depict Greek athletes in training. Athletic competition allowed the Greek city-states to play out their rivalries in a nonviolent way.*

*The priestess of the Temple of Apollo at Delphi—the so-called oracle (also known as the Pythia)—swoons as she prepares to deliver a divine message.*

was a rapid transition to monumental (large-scale) stone temples throughout the Greek sphere. Thereafter, from ancient Rome through the Renaissance to the modern world, Greek temple design, featuring rows of columns topped by a pitched roof, has remained the standard of architectural grandeur, serenity, and nobility.

All of the temples in the various city-states were viewed as sacred places, but a few held special significance and prestige for all Greeks no matter where they came from. Perhaps the most important of these Panhellenic temples were those dedicated to Athena and Apollo at Delphi, in central Greece, home of the famous oracle. The oracle was a priestess who, it was thought, conveyed prophecies from Apollo to humans. (The sacred site and the divine messages were also called oracles.)

Because of its unique and special attributes as a shrine, in late Archaic times Delphi became an independent town belonging to no city-state and protected by a religious council made up of representatives from many surrounding Greek states.

Thus, the Archaic Age witnessed the rise of two potent forces—fiercely independent city-states and Panhellenic activities and traditions. These forces often seemed to contradict or oppose each other. In spite of the depth of their shared language and culture, the poleis rarely got along or united in a common cause. The Archaic Greeks had no inkling that a major exception to this rule loomed on their horizon. Soon they would be forced to unite to defend their homes and way of life in what would prove the greatest challenge they had ever faced.

# Chapter 3

# Men of Marathon: The First Defeat of Persia

Although the Greeks developed a complex, thriving, and ambitious culture in the Archaic Age, they remained minor players on the world political stage. At the dawn of Greece's Classical Age, which began circa 500 B.C., a number of Mediterranean peoples were enjoying prosperity or growth and exerted considerable power in their respective spheres of influence; among them were the Phoenicians based in Palestine, the Carthaginians in North Africa, and the Etruscans, Samnites, and Romans in Italy. (By this time, large areas of southern Italy and the island of Sicily had been colonized by Greeks as well.)

None of these peoples as yet had a large empire. And none of their homelands compared in size, wealth, and influence with the Persian Empire, at the time by far the most extensive and powerful realm in the world. Persia had built its extensive empire only recently. In 559 B.C., a young nobleman from the small Persian homeland of Fars (in southern Iran), then a province of the Iranian state of Media, ascended the local throne as Cyrus II. In less than eight years, the ambitious and capable Cyrus led his people in a meteoric rise from obscurity. He defeated his Median masters, absorbed their empire, and then proceeded to expand his new realm even farther. Under his rule and that of his son and successor, Cambyses, the Persian Empire soon encompassed the entire Near East, including Egypt and Palestine, and stretched eastward to the borders of India.

One pivotal part of that great territorial expanse was Asia Minor, conquered by Cyrus in 546 B.C. Among the area's many local peoples who became Persian subjects at this time were the Greeks of Ionia, on the Aegean coast. This brought the cultures of East and West, and more specifically the Greeks and Persians, into direct contact for

*A modern drawing depicts Cyrus II (on the horse) as a young man.*

the first time. Tensions in conquered Ionia steadily escalated. Meanwhile, Cambyses' successor, Darius I, began to lay plans for extending his empire westward into Europe.

These events put the Persians and mainland Greeks on a collision course that would change the course of history. The Greco-Persian wars, which took place in stages from 499 to 479 B.C., resulted in a tremendous victory of the tiny Greek states over the Persian colossus. The *Marathonomachoi*, or "men of Marathon," the hoplites who defeated the first Persian expedition against the mainland, quickly became renowned throughout the known world. More importantly, almost overnight the Greeks as a whole became a world-class power to be reckoned with; they would remain the most influential single people in the West for three centuries to come.

## The Ionian Rebellion

The immediate series of events leading to the outbreak of the Greco-Persian wars began in 512 B.C. when King Darius led an army across the Bosporus Strait, separating Asia Minor from Europe. His goal was to conquer Scythia, the sparsely populated area lying west and northwest of the Black Sea. He had heard rumors of gold deposits there, but there is little doubt that he also desired to establish a foothold from which to launch more ambitious expeditions into Europe. Although Darius failed to capture Scythia, on the way back to Asia he conquered Thrace, the region lying directly north of the Aegean Sea. This gave him the European base camp he needed.

Darius did not pursue his dreams of westward expansion right away, however. For reasons that are unclear, he delayed for several years; in the meantime, he had to deal with unexpected trouble in Ionia. The Greek cities in that region had long been unhappy under Persian rule and longed to regain their freedom. According to military historian Philip de Souza:

The Ionians clearly resented having to obey tyrants who were appointed from among their fellow countrymen at the whim of a king whose court was far away and whose priorities rarely coincided with their own. Some of the Ionian cities and islands had been developing a form of democratic government when they came under Persian influence. Such developments continued in mainland Greece, especially in Athens, but the move toward popular participation in government was prematurely halted in Ionia. King Darius . . . demanded manpower for military expeditions and money . . . paid in silver. . . . The campaigns were against people like the Scythians, whom the Greeks could not possibly see as a threat to their own lands, and the silver was hoarded in distant Persia, or spent on gifts and wages for other foreigners. The Ionians got little in return for their annexation by the Persians. [18]

Hoping to correct what he and many other Ionians saw as an intolerable situation, in 499 B.C. Aristagoras, a leading citizen of Miletus,

the most prosperous Ionian city, instigated a rebellion. Most of the Ionian cities joined in and gladly threw out their puppet rulers.

Aristagoras was not so naive as to think that Darius would take this affront lightly. So the Milesian journeyed to the Greek mainland and tried to enlist the aid of Sparta, in the southern Peloponnesus, which had the strongest land army in the Greek sphere. Aristagoras tried to get one of Sparta's kings (two of which ruled jointly), Cleomenes, to agree to an invasion of Persia. But when Cleomenes learned how far away the Persian heartland was, he testily told his visitor: "You must leave Sparta by sunset. Your proposal to take Spartans [on] a three months' journey from the sea is a highly improper one." [19]

The disappointed Aristagoras went next to Athens, where the recently empowered democratic Assembly gave him a much warmer reception than Cleomenes had. The Athenians agreed to send aid, as did the citizens of Eretria (a polis lying in western Euboea, north of Athens). In 498 B.C., twenty Athenian ships and five Eretrian vessels, all loaded with troops and supplies, landed in Ionia. Not long afterward, Aristagoras himself led a raiding party of Milesians and Athenians inland to Sardis, Persia's local provincial capital, and torched the city. In the words of Herodotus, the fifth-century B.C. Greek historian whose *Histories* is the principal ancient source for the Greco-Persian wars, "One house was set alight by a soldier, and flames rapidly spread until the whole town was ablaze." [20]

When King Darius heard the news of the attack on Sardis, he expressed outrage

*This painting on a ceramic vessel shows a Persian messenger informing king Darius I of the Athenian attack on Sardis.*

that a group of puny states situated on the fringes of the civilized world (which in his mind was centered in Persia) had dared to challenge his authority. And he immediately vowed revenge on all involved. "He did not give a thought to the Ionians," Herodotus wrote,

> knowing perfectly well that the punishment for their revolt would come. But he asked who the Athenians were, and then, on being told, called for his bow. He took it, set an arrow on the string, shot it up into the air and cried: "Grant, O God, that I may punish the Athenians." Then he commanded one of his servants to repeat to him the words, "Master, remember the Athenians,"

three times, whenever he sat down to dinner.[21]

## Showdown at Marathon

In the following four years, the Persian monarch proceeded to punish the Ionians. He sent troops, who assaulted several Ionian cities and carried thousands of Greek children back to Persia to become servants in the royal court. To break the sea power of Miletus and its neighbors, Darius sent some six hundred warships. Near the small Aegean island of Lade, these vessels decisively defeated a fleet of about 350 Ionian vessels that had hastily assembled to meet the threat. Then a Persian land force laid siege to and captured Miletus. According to Herodotus, the Athenians, who had long had close ties with the Milesians, were particularly distressed by this event. When, soon afterward, a popular Athenian playwright produced a play titled *The Capture of Miletus,* Herodotus writes "the audience in the theater burst into tears. The author was fined a thousand drachmas for reminding them of a disaster which touched them so closely, and they forbade anybody ever to put the play on the stage again."[22]

The Athenians were upset not only for the Milesians but also for themselves, as there was widespread fear that Athens would become Darius's next target. This worry was well grounded. In 490 B.C. the Persian king was ready to achieve his revenge on

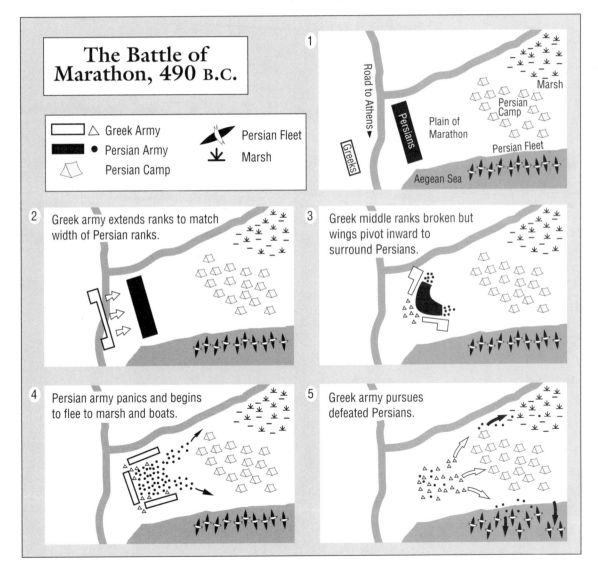

**The Battle of Marathon, 490 B.C.**

☐ △ Greek Army
■ ● Persian Army
⛺ Persian Camp
Persian Fleet
↓ Marsh

1. [Plain of Marathon map with Road to Athens, Persians, Greeks, Persian Camp, Marsh, Persian Fleet, Aegean Sea]

2. Greek army extends ranks to match width of Persian ranks.

3. Greek middle ranks broken but wings pivot inward to surround Persians.

4. Persian army panics and begins to flee to marsh and boats.

5. Greek army pursues defeated Persians.

Athens and Eretria and sent a large fleet of ships across the Aegean. Commanded by Darius's nephew, Artaphernes, and a general named Datis, the Persian army first landed on the western shore of Euboea and sacked Eretria.

In late summer, the Persian fleet crossed to Attica and landed at Marathon, a plain located about twenty-five miles northeast of the next target—Athens. Aboard one of the ships was the deposed Athenian tyrant Hippias, now an embittered old man, whom the Persians intended to install as their puppet after capturing Athens. At least twenty thousand Persian soldiers disembarked on the western end of the plain. Waiting for them on the eastern end, and blocking the road to Athens, was that city's entire citizen militia, a force of about nine thousand hoplites. They were soon joined by about one thousand hoplites from the tiny polis of Plataea, a neighbor and faithful ally of Athens. A tense standoff now ensued, as the opposing armies faced each other for several days. Finally, the Greeks decided that, despite the enemy's superior numbers, the best course was to attack.

The exact sequence of events in the battle, which may have occurred on September 12, remains somewhat unclear, in large part because Herodotus's account is rather vague. He does say that the Greeks reduced the number of ranks in their center so that their battle line could be extended to match the width of the Persian army. (That way the Persians could not outflank them, or move around their sides to their rear.) Combining Herodotus's account with other

literary and archaeological evidence, scholars have pieced together a likely scenario of the battle, summarized here by noted historian Peter Green. At the signal of a trumpet blast, he writes, the Greeks

moved forward, marching briskly, spears advanced. . . . As [they] came within range of the Persian archers (at about 150 yards distance), they broke into a [run], to get through the murderous rain of arrows as fast as possible, and engage [the enemy]. . . . Greek discipline, Greek tactics, [and] Greek weapons and body-armor were all very much superior to those of the Persians. . . . In the center, predictably, the Persians had the best of it. Step by hard-fought step . . . the Athenian hoplites were forced back. . . . Meanwhile on the wings the Greeks carried all before them. Many of the fleeing Persians stumbled into the Great Marsh [on the northeastern border of the plain] and were drowned. . . . At this critical point . . . the Athenian and Plataean wings [each constituting a small but powerful phalanx] about-faced . . . and [executed] a double-pincer movement [that trapped the Persian center between them]. . . . The tide of battle turned and the Persian line broke. Those who could forced their way through to the sea . . . where their ships were ready for departure. The Athenians pursued them closely, cutting down stragglers in the shallows till the water ran red with blood.[23]

# How Many Persians Fought at Marathon?

*In his informative book about the battle of Marathon, noted military historian Nicholas Sekunda attempts to estimate the number of Persian fighters who confronted the roughly ten thousand Athenians and Plataeans. He draws heavily on the fifth-century B.C. Greek historian Herodotus, as well as on modern studies.*

Our starting point for an estimate of Persian strength must be Herodotus's statement that the fleet numbered 600 triremes [oared warships]. . . . We know that if a trireme was fully manned with rowers it could carry a maximum of about 200 men—170 rowers and 30 others. So the absolute maximum number of humans the fleet could physically have transported was 120,000. . . . Herodotus records that . . . each trireme carried 30 Persians [who were fighters rather than rowers, and a few triremes of that era could carry 40 fighters]. This would give a total number of either 18,000 or 24,000 men. . . . The Persian army was organized into "thousands" [units] of 1,000 men and "myriads" of 10,000 men. I suggest that the main force of infantry at Marathon consisted of two [myriads, or a total of 20,000 fighters].

## Themistocles' Foresight

The numbers of dead on each side give some idea of the immensity of the Greek victory. Datis and Artaphernes lost at least 6,400 men, while only 192 Athenians were killed. The surviving Persians were forced to abandon their plans for establishing a European beachhead in Attica and returned in humiliation to Asia Minor. Meanwhile, as messages of congratulation flooded in from across the Greek world, Athens reveled in its newfound image as Greece's savior. The victorious "men of Marathon" were honored as national heroes and thereafter became models of the valorous Greek defending his home and way of life against the vile "barbarians" (then a common Greek term for non-Greeks).

Unfortunately for the Athenians, the great elation and pride they felt was accompanied by overconfidence. They and most other Greeks assumed that after such an embarrassing defeat the Persians would not dare to return. One Athenian considered this view shortsighted, however. Themistocles, one of the ten generals who had commanded at Marathon, was sure that Darius would seek vengeance with a much larger army and that Athens, and hopefully all of Greece, must be ready. Moreover, Themistocles foresaw that the key to both defense and offense against the Persians was a strong navy. When a rich

# Themistocles' Threat

*According to Plutarch in his biography of Themistocles (quoted here from Ian Scott-Kilvert's translation in* The Rise and Fall of Athens*), shortly before the battle of Salamis, another Greek leader told Themistocles that a man without a city (a reference to the recent evacuation of Athens) had no right to give advice and orders to men who still had cities. Themistocles angrily answered:*

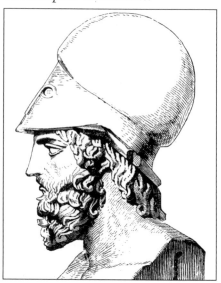

A drawing based on a bust that some claim depicts Themistocles.

It is quite true, you wretch, that we have given up our houses and our city walls, because we did not choose to become enslaved for the sake of things that have no life or soul. But what we still possess is the greatest city in all Greece, our 200 ships of war, which are ready now to defend you, if you are still willing to be saved by them.

*In his Histories (Aubrey de Sélincourt's translation), Herodotus reported that Themistocles added this threat:*

If you refuse [to take my advice], we will immediately put our families aboard and sail for Italy. . . . Where will you be without the Athenian fleet? When you have lost it, you will remember my words.

vein of silver was discovered in southern Attica a few years after Marathon, he convinced the Assembly (against strong opponents who wanted to divide up the windfall among the citizens) to build a fleet. "The result," said Plutarch in his biography of Themistocles,

was that the Athenians built a hundred triremes [oared warships] with the money. . . . After this he continued to draw the Athenians little by little and turn their thoughts in the direction of the sea. He told them that . . . with the power they would command in their fleet they could not only drive off the barbarians, but become the leaders of all Greece. [24]

As it turned out, Themistocles had been right about Darius's desire to punish the

Greeks. After the debacle at Marathon, the Persian king "was more than ever determined to make war on Greece," as Herodotus put it.

Without loss of time he dispatched couriers to the various states under his dominion with orders to raise an army much larger than before; and also warships, transports, horses, and grain. So the royal command went round; and all Asia was in an uproar for three years, with the best men being enrolled in the army for the invasion of Greece. [25]

Darius did not live to see his revenge fulfilled, however. He died in 486 B.C. and his son, Xerxes (ZERK-seez), ended up leading the new expedition into Europe. In 480 B.C. the new Persian king marched westward at the head of the largest invasion force assembled anywhere in the world in ancient times. It consisted of an estimated 200,000 combat infantry and cavalry; 800 to 1,000 ships manned by at least 150,000 oarsmen and sailors; and a huge company of support personnel and camp followers numbering perhaps as many as 300,000.

## At the Gates of Fire

Many of the poleis of northern Greece were so terrified of this enormous horde that they surrendered without a fight. In contrast, most of the major southern city-states put aside their differences and, led by Athens and Sparta, prepared to resist the invaders. The Greek plan, which followed Themistocles'

advice, was to attempt to destroy the Persian fleet. Without its vast stores of supplies, the Persian land army could not sustain itself for very long.

To buy time in which to assemble a united Greek fleet, a small force of hoplites hurried to the pass of Thermopylae (about a hundred miles northwest of Athens), through which Xerxes planned to enter southern

*Attacking Persian soldiers are driven back by the Greek defenders at Thermopylae.*

Greece. At this narrow defile, the so-called Gates of Fire, the Spartan king Leonidas and his personal bodyguard of three hundred men took their positions. Backing them up were soldiers from Corinth, Thebes, Thespiae, and other nearby states, making a total of about seven thousand. Though the Persians outnumbered them by nearly thirty to one, only a few of Xerxes' men could enter the pass at one time, and these the hoplites proceeded to butcher in wave after wave.

For three days, the intrepid band of Greeks held the pass against the enemy host. Finally, however, a local man succumbed to the temptation of Persian gold and led a contingent of Xerxes' troops along a little-known mountain path toward the rear of the Greek position. Discovering that he would soon be outflanked, Leonidas ordered most of the Greeks to leave. He and his Spartans stayed, along with a few hundred Thespians and a handful of others, to delay the enemy as long as possible. Finally surrounded, the defenders fought with courage and determination that has become legendary. "Many of the invaders fell," Herodotus wrote, while

behind them their company commanders plied their whips . . . driving the men on. Many [Persians] fell into the

## The Order to Evacuate Athens

*These excerpts from the decree announcing the evacuation of Athens in the face of the approaching Persian army, an order instigated by Themistocles, are from A.J. Podlecki's translation in his definitive biography of that controversial figure.*

It was decreed . . . on the motion of Themistocles, son of Neocles . . . to entrust the city of Athens, Athens's guardian [Athena], and all the other gods, for safekeeping and to resist the barbarian for the land's sake. The Athenians themselves . . . shall deposit their children and wives in Troizen [an area lying to the southwest] . . . and deposit the old men and possessions in Salamis [an island near Athens]. The temple-treasurers and priestesses shall stay on the Acropolis to protect the property of the gods. All the other Athenians . . . who are of age shall embark on the two hundred ships which have been prepared and shall fight the barbarian both for their own freedom and for that of the rest of the Greeks. . . . In order that all Athenians may present a united front to the barbarian, those who have withdrawn from the country [i.e., have been banished] for ten years are to go to Salamis and remain there until a decree [of amnesty] is passed about them.

sea and were drowned, and still more were trampled to death by their friends. No one could count the number of the dead. The Greeks . . . put forth all their strength and fought with fury and desperation. By this time most of their spears were broken. . . . [They] took up a position . . . on the little hill at the entrance to the pass. . . . Here they resisted to the last, with their swords, if they had them, and, if not, with their hands and teeth, until the Persians . . . finally overwhelmed them with [arrows].[26]

For Xerxes, it was a hollow victory. Heaped beside the bodies of Leonidas and his brave comrades were the corpses of nearly twenty thousand Persians.

## Divine Salamis

Xerxes had another hollow victory in store for him when he reached Athens on or about September 17, 480 B.C. The city was largely deserted. Themistocles had convinced his fellow Athenians to leave behind their homes and material belongings, since it made no sense "to become enslaved for the sake of things that have no life or soul."[27]

As the Persians torched the city, they did not know that the Athenians and other Greeks were preparing for a major sea battle. Following a plan devised by Themistocles, the allied fleet of about 340 ships assembled in the narrow strait between the island of Salamis and mainland Attica. (A recent prophecy from the Delphic Oracle had stated, "Divine Salamis, you will bring

*Greek warships wreak havoc among the Persian vessels at Salamis.*

death to women's sons."[28] How much this influenced the decision to fight at Salamis is unknown.) Believing he would be victorious, Xerxes watched from a nearby hill as 600 of his own ships moved into the strait.

That day the fate of Europe was decided; and as Xerxes realized to his dismay, its future did not belong to Persia. "The Persians could bring only a small part of their whole fleet into action at a time," Plutarch recalled, "as their ships constantly fouled one another in the narrow straits." In great bursts of speed, the Greek triremes rammed and sunk the enemy vessels. "And the Greeks finally put them to utter rout."[29] Fortunately, an eyewitness account of the battle has survived, penned by the Athenian playwright Aeschylus, who fought at Salamis (as well as at Marathon). *The Persians* (produced eight years later) contains a section in which, following the battle, a Persian messenger tells Xerxes' mother:

> From the Greek ships rose like a song of joy the piercing battle-cry, and from the island crags echoed an answering shout. The Persians knew their error; fear gripped every man. They were no fugitives who sang that terrifying paean [battle hymn], but Greeks charging with courageous hearts to battle. . . . At once ship into ship battered its brazen beak. A Greek ship charged first, and chopped off the whole stern of a Persian galley. Then charge followed charge on every side. At first by its huge impetus our fleet withstood them. But soon, in that narrow space, our ships were jammed in hundreds; none could help another. They rammed each other

*The Spartans take the forward position in the Greek ranks at Plataea. The Greeks drove the Persians back to their camp and utterly destroyed it.*

with their prows of bronze; and some were stripped of every oar. Meanwhile the enemy came round us in a ring and charged. Our vessels heeled over; the sea was hidden, carpeted with wrecks and dead men; all the shores and reefs were full of dead. Then every ship we had broke rank and rowed for life. The Greeks seized fragments of wrecks and broken oars and hacked and stabbed at our men swimming in the sea. . . . The whole sea was one din of shrieks and dying groans, till night and darkness hid the scene. . . . Never before in one day died so vast a company of men.[30]

## One Door Closes, Another Opens

Following the slaughter at Salamis, Xerxes no doubt realized that his personal security could no longer be guaranteed. So he hastily boarded a ship and returned to Asia Minor. However, he left his son-in-law, Mardonius, with 150,000 troops, which both men felt was more than enough to subdue the tiny Greek states. This turned out to be another Persian miscalculation. The following spring, 479 B.C., hoplites from across the Greek mainland converged on Mardonius's army near Plataea and crushed it. A few days later, a Greek force took the Persians by surprise at Mycale, in Ionia, and sent them into a wild retreat.

For Xerxes and his successors, a door had closed forever. Never again would a Persian army attempt to enter Europe or pose a credible threat to the West. For the Greeks, by contrast, a door had opened, one through which they would now step, filled with confidence and vigor, into the blazing light of their most productive and memorable age.

# Imperial Athens: Its Golden Age and Rivalry with Sparta

T heir defeat of the Persian Empire instilled in the Greeks a feeling of enormous achievement. They had shown the world, as well as themselves, that, like their ancestors at Troy, they were capable of glorious deeds. Moreover, the stunning victory over the immense forces of Darius and Xerxes seemed only a first step toward other significant accomplishments. In this way, as historian W.G. Hardy memorably puts it, the victory over Persia became "the torch to set fire to the brilliance of the great age of the Greeks. There was a tremendous upswelling of confidence . . . [and now they] felt that there was nothing they could not attempt." [31]

This confidence was certainly a major part of the spirit that drove the Greeks, par-

ticularly the Athenians, during the first half-century that followed the Persian invasions. Greeks of later generations came to call this remarkable period the *Pentekontaetia,* the "Fifty Years." In that relatively short span, Athens produced a cultural outburst that included some of the finest architecture, sculpture, and drama ever created. It also spread democratic institutions and cultural ideas to other Greek states. "Never in the history of the world," Chester Starr remarks, "have so few people done so much in the space of two or three generations." [32] Today, the Fifty Years is often called the golden age of Athens or the "Age of Pericles," in reference to the most influential Athenian leader of that era. It was Pericles who, sensing Athens's unique attributes and achievements, predicted with amazing foresight: "Future ages will wonder at us, as the present age wonders at us now." [33]

Yet the Fifty Years had a darker side that tempered and sometimes tarnished its brighter, more admirable aspects. First, the period witnessed complex political turmoil and sporadic but bloody military strife among the Greek states. Also, Athens paid for its lavish cultural endeavors largely by exploiting the city-states that made up the rapidly assembled maritime empire it held together by means of naked force.

Finally, and most ominously, the Fifty Years was shaped more than anything else by a rivalry between Greece's two strongest states—Athens and Sparta. Their sharp cultural differences, mutual distrust, and political and military disputes ultimately and sadly overshadowed the creative output of the age. The growing animosity between imperial Athens, its nemesis Sparta, and their respective leagues of allies eventually led to the outbreak of the Peloponnesian War in 431 B.C. This devastating conflict brought the productivity of the Fifty Years to a crashing halt and ravaged the Greek world for nearly three decades. Thus, the first half of the Classical Age (ca. 500–404 B.C., encompassing the Greco-Persian wars, the Fifty Years, and the Peloponnesian War) ended with almost all of the city-states exhausted and bitter.

*The architect Ictinus shows Pericles the plans for a new building. Pericles closely supervised the building programs he sponsored.*

## The Delian League

Clearly, the crucial fifth century B.C. began with more optimism and hope than it ended with. Thucydides, the Athenian soldier and historian who chronicled the Peloponnesian War for posterity, summarized the situation that prevailed in Greece directly following the expulsion of the Persians in 479 B.C. The Greeks "split into two divisions," he wrote, "one group following Athens and the other Sparta." Yet "for a short time the war-time alliance held together." [34] During these few years of peace among the Greek states, Athens immediately attempted to assert its influence and leadership among its neighbors. Few Greeks were surprised, since the Athenians had become an outgoing, forceful, and ambitious people. According to Thucydides, an observer from Corinth said of them:

> An Athenian is always an innovator, quick to form a resolution and quick at carrying it out. . . . They will take risks

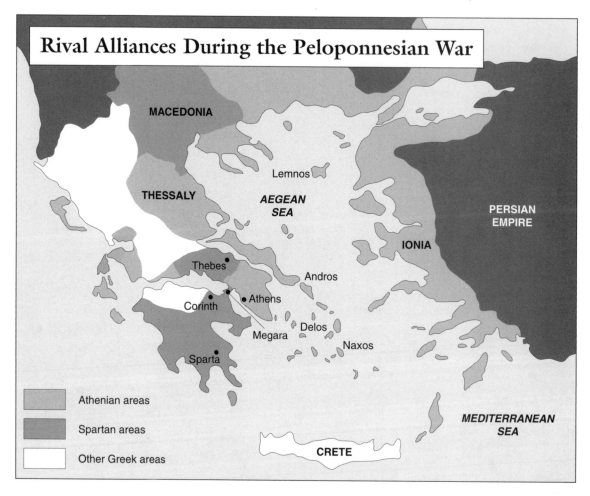

**Rival Alliances During the Peloponnesian War**

MACEDONIA

THESSALY

Lemnos

AEGEAN SEA

PERSIAN EMPIRE

IONIA

Thebes

Andros

Corinth

Athens

Megara

Delos

Naxos

Sparta

Athenian areas

Spartan areas

Other Greek areas

MEDITERRANEAN SEA

CRETE

# How Athens's Democracy Worked

Under Pericles, the Athenian democracy established by Cleisthenes grew stronger and more open. Most governmental authority was vested in the citizen Assembly, and the decisions and directives made by that body were carried out by the city's magistrates (public administrators) and the Council (*Boule*). The Council was made up of five hundred legislators chosen by lot (random selection). It drew up recommendations, in effect legislative bills dealing with state business and the community in general. These bills then went to the Assembly, whose members debated and voted on them. If a majority voted for a bill, it became a decree with the force of law. The Assembly could also change a bill by adding amendments or by sending it back to the Council to be reframed; or the voters could reject the bill outright. The Council also made sure that the decisions made by the Assembly were duly carried out by overseeing the financial and other administrative business of the community. This task was accomplished by various Council subcommittees (boards of councilors), which closely supervised the magistrates. The magistrates, who actually ran state affairs on a daily basis, included nine administrators (the archons) and ten generals (the *strategoi*), elected annually by the Assembly.

against their better judgment, and still, in the midst of danger, remain confident. . . . If they win a victory, they follow it up at once, and if they suffer a defeat, they scarcely fall back at all. . . . If they aim at something and do not get it, they think they have been deprived of what belonged to them already; whereas, if their enterprise is successful, they regard that success as nothing compared to what they will do next. [35]

This confident, resilient spirit at least partly explains the bold moves Athens made. It insisted that, to protect Greece from any further Persian incursions, a formal alliance of city-states should be created. In the winter of 487–486 B.C., the Athenians organized and presided over a meeting of delegates from more than 150 mainland, island, and Ionian poleis. Their alliance came to be called the Delian League, after Delos, the tiny Aegean island where the congress took place. This was the federation's common name. Its official name, used less often, was "the Athenians and Their Allies," which was more revealing of its true nature. On paper, it was an alliance of equals, but in reality, Athens, which had by far the largest and strongest navy in Greece, ran the show.

In time, the Athenians were unable to resist taking advantage of their powerful position as head of the league. When, in 469 B.C., the island polis of Naxos tried to withdraw from the organization, which was its legal right, Athens treated it like a rebellious subject. Athenian warships attacked Naxos and confiscated its small fleet. Other similar incidents followed. The Athenians, said Thucydides, "made themselves unpopular by bringing the severest pressure to bear on allies," and forced "back into the alliance any state that wanted to leave it." [36] In this way, Athens became an imperial power. And it grew increasingly wealthy from the dues paid by the league members, which eventually amounted to little more than tribute (payment made by one party to acknowledge its submission to another).

Many people today may find it strange that Athens could become an imperial power when it had such an open democracy. It must be kept in mind, however, that the citizens who voted in the Athenian Assembly were more concerned with their own rights than with those of neighboring states. Also, persuasive orators with their own agendas could and often did sway the voters to endorse overly aggressive and morally questionable policies. As Charles Freeman points out:

Democratic government did not necessarily mean benign or tolerant government. Decrees of the Assembly included those ordering the massacre of the entire male population of another Greek island [Melos] and the mass enslavement of its women and children.

Pericles unscrupulously diverted the tribute raised by the empire . . . into his building program[s]. . . . The city that had defined and upheld the concept of sovereignty of the Greek city against the onslaught of the Persians abused and even destroyed the independence of other Greek cities. It is with these paradoxes in mind that the [creative] achievements of classical Athens must be explored. [37]

## The Classic Achievement

The culmination and most visible aspect of Athens's creative activities in this period was an extensive construction program that reached its peak in the 440s and 430s B.C. with the erection of the Parthenon and other temples on the Acropolis. The driving force behind these projects was Pericles, who had been born about 495 B.C. into the same aristocratic family that had produced the democratic reformer Cleisthenes. In 461, following the assassination of the popular democratic leader Ephialtes, Pericles emerged as Athens's most influential politician and an ardent champion of open democracy (although simultaneously an advocate of Athenian domination of the Delian League).

Pericles felt that, as an emerging world power, Athens needed to erect imposing buildings and other monuments befitting its status as Greece's leading state. "I declare that our city is an education to Greece," he is credited as saying later.

Athens, alone of the states we know . . . [possesses] a greatness that surpasses what was imagined of her. . . . You should fix your eyes every day on the greatness of Athens as she really is, and should fall in love with her. When you realize her greatness, then reflect that what made her great was men with a spirit of adventure. [38]

The Athenians responded to such words with enormous pride, energy, and industriousness. In a few short years they transformed the drab summit of the Acropolis, still strewn with the rubble from the structures burned by the Persians a generation before, into a temple complex of unprecedented splendor and breathtaking beauty. These new buildings not only served as effective propaganda for Athens in Pericles' own time but became eternal symbols of Greek cultural achievement. Writing some five centuries later, when Greece was under Roman rule, Plutarch exclaimed:

There was one measure above all which . . . adorned [Athens] and created amazement among the rest of mankind, and which is today the sole testimony that the tales of the ancient power and glory of Greece are no mere fables. By this I mean his construction of temples and public buildings. . . . They were created in so short a span, and yet for all time. . . . A bloom of eternal freshness hovers over these works . . . and preserves them from the touch of time, as if some unfading spirit of youth, some ageless vitality had been breathed into them. [39]

When the Acropolis complex was completed, a grand stone staircase led up the western side of the hill. Perched on a stone platform on one side of the stairway was the tiny Temple of Athena Nike, graceful and elegant in its own right but providing a

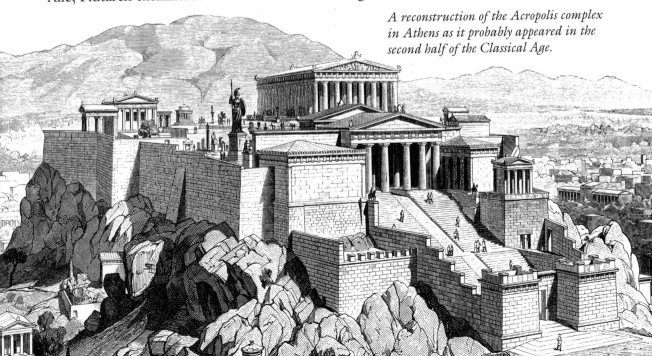

*A reconstruction of the Acropolis complex in Athens as it probably appeared in the second half of the Classical Age.*

mere foretaste of the wonders beyond. At the top of the staircase loomed the Propylaea, a massive and magnificent column-lined entranceway leading onto the summit. Beyond this portal sprawled the heart of the complex—a mass of temples, outdoor shrines and altars, walkways of polished marble, and magnificent bronze and stone statues.

The summit of the Acropolis was dominated, however, by the Parthenon, dedicated to the city's patron, Athena. Designed

*A model shows the interior of the Parthenon in its original glory.*

by the architect Ictinus and sculptor Phidias, it was 237 feet long, 110 feet wide, and some 65 feet high, and it incorporated over 22,000 tons of polished marble. Inside stood Phidias's awesome statue of Athena, which was nearly forty feet high and decorated with ivory and pure gold.

In addition to timeless art and architecture, Athens produced a dramatic output of incomparable excellence in the Fifty Years. The Athenians had invented the institution of the theater in the late 500s B.C. During Pericles' youth, the art of drama matured, and in the generation that followed some of the greatest plays ever written were presented at the Theater of Dionysus, which rested at the foot of the Acropolis. These included works by Aeschylus, Sophocles, and Euripides, who wrote tragedies, and Aristophanes, a comic playwright, among others. Somehow, this handful of gifted individuals managed to create, in a stroke, the model for great drama and theater for all times.

Thanks to the drawing power of these writers, Athens's main drama festival, the City Dionysia, developed into a major holiday attraction spanning several days at the end of March. All Greeks were welcome to attend, and people journeyed from far and wide to see the plays. (Nevertheless, only Athenian playwrights were allowed to compete for prizes.) The Athenian government naturally took advantage of this unique attraction, as it did with the Acropolis complex, to show off the city's growing wealth, cultural finery, and creative genius. The state maintained the theater building, paid the actors (and possi-

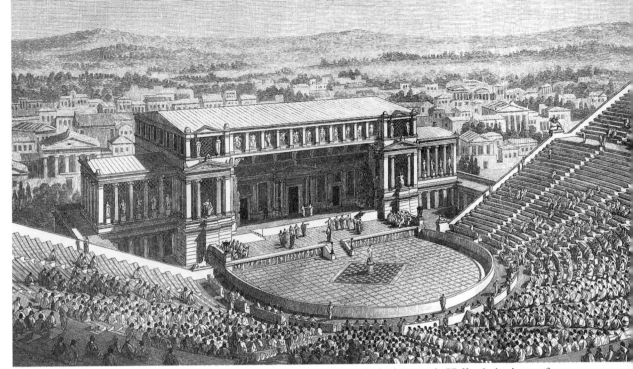

*The Theater of Dionysus nestled at the foot of the Acropolis, as it looked in early Hellenistic times after numerous renovations.*

bly the playwrights), and provided the prizes for the dramatic contests. All other expenses of play production, including costumes, sets, musicians, and so forth, were the responsibility of the backers, well-to-do citizens the state asked to help support the festival.

## Sparta's Armed Camp

It is likely that among the crowds attending the plays at the Theater of Dionysus few Spartans could be found. This was not simply because Athens and Sparta were often enemies. The fact was that Sparta's political and social institutions and cultural attitudes were not only highly atypical for a Greek state but also frequently the polar opposite of those of Athens. When someone visited Periclean Athens, they found a grand, impressive place that was open to the world and welcomed new ideas and debate. In contrast, to the out-

side world Sparta appeared small, unadorned, and off the beaten path, an image that belied its real power and influence. As Thucydides put it, if Sparta

> were to become deserted and only the temples and foundations of buildings remained, I think that future generations would, as time passed, find it very difficult to believe that the place had really been as powerful as it was represented to be. Yet the Spartans . . . stand at the head not only of the whole Peloponnesus itself but also of numerous allies beyond its frontiers. Since, however, the city . . . contains no temples or monuments of great magnificence, but is simply a collection of villages . . . its appearance would not come up to expectation.[40]

*Spartan youths train in a gymnasium. Young Spartan men endured an extensive, years-long training program designed to make them fearsome warriors.*

Why did the influential Spartans prefer a modest, almost secluded existence and reject most artistic endeavors and material luxuries in favor of simple necessities? The general answer is that they maintained a politically backward and socially repressive society. By the advent of the Classical Age, most other Greek states had long since gotten rid of kinglike chiefs and instituted oligarchies or democracies. Sparta, however, retained its royalty, with two kings ruling jointly at all times. They were not all-powerful, though; their authority was outweighed in all but religious and military matters by a group of elders called ephors.

The society this elite group of men oversaw was built completely around the *agoge*, a harsh, regimented system of practices intended to turn out strong, effective warriors for Sparta's renowned and feared army. The ephors examined all male infants. Those considered too weak were left outside on a mountainside to die. Spartan boys who made it past this initial test faced years of difficult, relentless training in which they learned to endure all manner of hardships. "To toughen their feet," Sarah Pomeroy and her colleagues write,

they went barefoot, and they often went naked as well. When they were 12, their hair was cut short. [They] were each allocated only one cloak yearly to wear in all kinds of weather. . . . The boys slept in groups on rough mats that they had made themselves. To develop cunning and self-reliance, they were encouraged to supplement their food rations by stealing. Whipping awaited anyone who revealed his lack of skill by getting caught. . . . From the ages of 14 to 20 [they] performed their preliminary military service. . . . Between the ages of 20 and 30 they were permitted to marry but had to continue to live with their army groups until the age of 30.[41]

One of the major reasons the *agoge* developed was to maintain the tightest security possible to keep Sparta's agricultural serfs, called Helots, in line. These serfs were the former inhabitants of the neighboring state of Messenia, which the Spartans had conquered in the seventh century B.C. The Helots greatly outnumbered native Spartans and the threat of rebellion was ever present. Consequently, as Paul Cartledge, the leading scholar of ancient Sparta, says:

> The Spartans responded by turning themselves into a sort of permanently armed camp. . . . Male Spartan citizens were forbidden any other trade, profession, or business than war, and . . . had to be on a constant state of alert and readiness, for enemies within as well as without.[42]

It is no wonder, then, that the Spartans distrusted change and preferred to avoid

# The Spartan Tremblers

*"The accusation of being a coward was the most damning that could be made against a true Spartan,"* scholar Philip de Souza points out in his account of the Greco-Persian wars. Spartan boys who could not endure the rigors of the* agoge *and Spartan men who refused to fight or ran away in battle were called* tresantes, *or tremblers. De Souza continues:*

They were despised because they were the very opposite of the Spartan hoplite ideal. Tremblers were required to wear colored patches on their red cloaks to distinguish them and they were shunned by the rest of the [Spartan soldiers]. Their own messmates . . . would have nothing to do with them, even to the point of refusing to speak to them. They could not hold any of the public offices and were unable to gain justice for insults or injuries, nor could they make legal agreements with other Spartans. No Spartan would allow his daughter to marry a trembler . . . [and] no one would want to marry their children to the sons or daughters of a trembler.

contact with most other Greek states, especially those they viewed as too liberal and unstable, like Athens.

## Threats to the Balance of Power

Because of the many political and cultural differences between Athens and Sparta, confrontation between these two leading Greek states was probably inevitable. The truce between them following the victory over Persia became increasingly uneasy. And when Athens punished Naxos and other Delian League members in the early 460s B.C., the Spartans saw the emerging Athenian empire as a dangerous threat to the balance of power in Greece. Sparta's Peloponnesian ally, Corinth, also grew fearful, as well as envious, of Athens. Corinthian maritime markets, once the richest in Greece, had been steadily shrinking thanks to the growing Athenian stranglehold on Aegean trade. As

a result, Corinth begged Sparta to intervene and cut Athens down to size.

Sparta may have been contemplating such action. But in the late 460s B.C. it suffered a devastating earthquake that flattened most of its houses. Taking advantage of this misfortune, the Helots revolted. And it took the Spartans more than five years to defeat the rebels and recover from the effects of the quake.

Meanwhile, Sparta kept a close eye on what was happening outside its borders. In 458 B.C. Athens defeated Corinth in a large sea battle, an event the Spartans viewed as ominous. That same year, Pericles further angered Sparta by beginning to erect the so-called Long Walls, which connected Athens's urban center to its port, Piraeus, about five miles away. These barriers created a safe access corridor to the sea and seemed to make Athens impervious to Spartan attack. In response, the following year the Spartans

*The Long Walls stretch from Piraeus toward Athens's urban center (in the distance).*

joined forces with the Thebans and fought the Athenians and some of their own allies at Tanagra, near Thebes. The Spartan side won a slim victory. But feeling they lacked the resources to enter Attica and besiege a city the size of Athens, the Spartans did not follow up their win.

In 446 B.C. the ongoing rivalry between Athens and Sparta quieted somewhat with the signing of a treaty known as the Thirty Years' Peace. The Athenians agreed to stay out of Peloponnesian affairs, and the Spartans grudgingly recognized the reality of Athens's empire. The parties also agreed to maintain a balance of power in which the Greek sphere would remain permanently divided between two large blocs of poleis—those backing Athens and those supporting Sparta.

The peace did not last thirty years, however, in large degree because Athens once again began interfering in the affairs of other states. In 433 B.C. it became embroiled in another dispute with Corinth and handed it another defeat. And the following year the Athenians boldly blockaded the port of their neighbor Megara, a Spartan ally. This was the last straw for the Spartans, who declared war in 431, initiating the most destructive conflict the Greek world had yet seen. Indeed, writes Donald Kagan, an authority on the war:

From the perspective of the fifth-century [B.C.] Greeks, the Peloponnesian War was legitimately perceived as a world war, causing enormous destruc-tion of life and property, intensifying factional and class hostility, and divid-ing the Greek states internally and destabilizing their relationships to one another. . . . [It] was also a conflict of unprecedented brutality . . . breaking through the thin line that separates civ-ilization from savagery. Anger, frus-tration, and the desire for vengeance increased as the fighting dragged on, resulting in a progression of atrocities that included maiming and killing cap-tured opponents. [43]

The war lasted for twenty-seven gruel-ing years. At first, the Athenians adopted a strategy of hiding behind the city walls and Long Walls and allowing their fleet to keep them well supplied with grain from the Greek cities ringing the Black Sea. This back-fired in a number of ways, however. The Spartans had free rein to ravage Athens's farmland and villages, and when a deadly plague struck the city, it spread rapidly in the crowded conditions and wiped out thou-sands of people. Sparta eventually con-structed its own fleet (largely financed with Persian gold) and cut off Athens's vital route to the Black Sea. In 404 B.C. Athens had no choice but to surrender. The Athenian hege-mony (dominance) of Greece had ended and a Spartan one had begun. At the time, no one could have guessed how briefly Sparta would maintain its preeminence or that all of the city-states would soon face a potent new threat from an unexpected quarter.

# Macedonia Eclipses the City-States

The ruinous Peloponnesian War and its aftermath had long-term consequences that adversely affected both the winners and losers in ways they did not foresee. First, the death and devastation wrought by the conflict caused widespread misery on all sides. The economic consequences included the wholesale destruction of farmhouses, farming implements, livestock, vines, and olive trees in many parts of Greece and the disruption of trade, both by land and by sea. Depopulation also took a toll. Tens of thousands of soldiers and sailors perished, leaving their wives and children to fend for themselves; as many as fifty thousand Athenians died of the plague; and the inhabitants of some cities were almost totally wiped out.

No less damaging to the city-states was the reality that the long and calamitous war had not taught them the lesson of unity. In the years following the conflict, bitterness and continued mutual distrust led to more fighting, as well as opportunistic foreign relations in which allies were easily made and just as easily discarded. As Thomas Martin puts it:

The first half of the fourth century [B.C.] saw frequently shifting alliances among the Greek city-states. Whichever ones happened to be weaker at a particular moment would temporarily join together against whichever city-state happened to be the strongest, only to lose their unity once the common enemy had been humbled. . . . All the efforts of the various major states to extend their hegemony over mainland Greece in the first half of the fourth century therefore ended in failure. By the mid 350s B.C., no Greek city-state had the power to rule more than itself on a consistent basis. The struggle for supremacy in Greece that had begun eighty years earlier with the outbreak of the Peloponnesian War had finally ended in a stalemate of exhaustion. [44]

The major Greek states were not only exhausted but, as a whole, more vulnerable than they had been in living memory. The many years of disunity and destruction had, in Donald Kagan's words, "ultimately weakened their capacity to resist conquest from outside." [45] This time the threat did not come from an Asian empire, however. Instead, the culprit was a Greek-speaking land—the kingdom of Macedonia (bordering the northwest corner of the Aegean). That state's capable and ambitious new king, Philip II, swiftly ended the era of city-state supremacy and opened the way for the Greeks to seek new horizons in western Asia.

## The March of the Ten Thousand

In a way that few appreciated at the time, the first major military event of the post–Peloponnesian War period foreshadowed both the decline of the city-states and Greece's exploitation of the Near East. A Persian prince known as Cyrus the Younger wanted to usurp the throne from his broth-er, Artaxerxes. In 401 B.C. Cyrus collected an army of Persian supporters, strengthened it by hiring ten thousand Greek mercenaries, and marched to Cunaxa, near Babylon (in what is now Iraq). Though Cyrus was defeated, the Greeks acquitted themselves well and suffered few casualties. But now they found themselves stranded and surrounded by hostile forces in the heart of Persia. Against incredible odds, they fought their way to the Black Sea and safety, a harrowing journey that the historian Xenophon, one of their number, chronicled in his *Anabasis* (meaning "march up-country").

This incident was significant in two ways. First, Xenophon and his comrades

*A surviving likeness of Macedonia's ambitious and talented King Philip II.*

represented a whole generation of men who, because of the long Peloponnesian War, knew little else but soldiering. In a sense they formed a mobile polis unto themselves, and soldiers of fortune and professional armies for hire (in contrast with local militias fighting to defend home and hearth) became increasingly prevalent. Second, the success of the Ten Thousand, as they came to be known, demonstrated to Greeks everywhere that the huge Persian Empire was vulnerable. If a small and ill-supplied Greek army could fight its way through Asia and emerge in one piece, the thinking went, what damage might a far larger and better supplied Greek force inflict on Persia?

With questions like this in mind, a group of influential Greek orators began to call for the Greek states to unite in a Panhellenic crusade against Persia. The best known of these orators, Isocrates, declared in 380 B.C. "Consider what a disgrace it is to sit idly by and see Asia flourishing more than Europe and the barbarians enjoying a greater prosperity than the Greeks. . . . We must not allow this state of affairs to go on."[46]

## The Rise of Thebes

For the time being, however, no such united Greek crusade was feasible thanks to the bickering and rivalries that continued among the major city-states. In the wake of its victory over Athens in the great war, Sparta enjoyed political and military dominance in Greece. But the Spartans were not very good at diplomacy and tended to get their way by using intimidation and force,

which caused much animosity among the states Sparta dealt with. Constantly fearful of these states forming anti-Spartan alliances, Sparta worried most about the Boeotian League, a confederation of about a dozen small poleis clustered around the larger state of Thebes. "This move towards Boeotian

*The men of the Ten Thousand rejoice upon reaching the safety of the Black Sea.*

# Theban Patriots Retake the Cadmea

*In his* Life of Pelopidas *(translated by Ian Scott-Kilvert in* The Age of Alexander*), Plutarch tells how the Theban hero Pelopidas and his comrades retook the Cadmea (Thebes's acropolis) from the Spartans who had occupied it. The patriots disguised themselves as women, infiltrated a party attended by those Thebans who were collaborating with the Spartans, and slew the traitors.*

They also called upon the citizens of Thebes to fight for their liberty. [They] armed all who came to them . . . breaking open the shops of the spearmakers and swordsmiths in the neighborhood. [The noted Theban] Epaminondas . . . joined them with a band of armed followers consisting of young men and the most active of the [military] veterans. By this time, the whole city was in an uproar, the air was filled with shouting . . . and men ran frantically here and there. . . . [Soon the insurgents] blockaded the Cadmea and attacked it on every side. . . . The Spartans surrendered on terms [that they be] allowed to depart [unharmed]. . . . It would be hard to find another instance in which so small a group of men with such weak resources overcame so numerous and powerful an enemy by virtue of sheer courage and determination.

unification," noted scholar Michael Grant explains,

> was a significant experiment in a type of inter-state union which generally eluded the Greeks of the classical period, with ultimate fatal results. But the new League could not—except perhaps theoretically—be regarded as an association of equals, since the Thebans, who became more prosperous and numerous after the Peloponnesian War, were always dominant.[47]

In fact, the Spartans feared the potential power of the Boeotian League so much that they audaciously declared it dissolved in 386 B.C. In an even more aggressive move, four years later about fifteen hundred Spartan hoplites occupied the Theban acropolis (the Cadmea) in support of a Spartan-backed coup of Thebes's democratic government. Not surprisingly, this heightened the already existing local hatred of Sparta and inspired patriotic resistance. In 379 B.C. a leading Theban named Pelopidas led a daring insurrection that forced the Spartans out of the city and restored democracy. Soon afterward, the Boeotian League was restored as well.

Thus, Spartan leaders once more found themselves fretting about the Theban confederation's potential to challenge their domination of Greek affairs. In the meantime, Thebes's neighbor, Athens, further complicated matters. First, the Athenians defiantly restored the Long Walls and built up another alliance of states similar to, though much smaller than, the Delian League. (Unlike the former confederation, the new one recognized the autonomy of all members and demanded no tribute.) Second, Athens and Thebes formed an alliance intended to discourage Spartan intrusions into Attica and Boeotia.

But Sparta was not so easily dissuaded and in the next few years continued to threaten Thebes. What Spartan leaders did not appreciate was that during this period the Theban military was in the midst of a major overhaul. Overseeing the reforms was a leading citizen named Epaminondas, aided by the popular patriot Pelopidas. Pelopidas took charge of the Sacred Band, a unit of three hundred elite fighters, each of whom was a match for the best Spartan hoplite.

Meanwhile, Epaminondas drilled the Theban phalanx in some new and unusual battlefield tactics. He had carefully observed the traditional way that Greek generals had arranged their infantry and noted that they placed their best troops on the right wing of the phalanx. When two opposing phalanxes clashed, the strong right wings always faced weaker enemy left wings, and the army with the most powerful right wing was usually able to crush the opposing left wing and then outflank and thereby defeat the other army. Epaminondas shrewdly reversed this battle order. He placed his weakest troops on his right wing and put his strongest men on the left. He also made his ranks fifty deep (compared with the Spartans' twelve ranks) and supported them with Thebes's crack unit, the Sacred Band.

The test of this new Theban army came in July 371 B.C. when the Spartan king Cleombrotus invaded Boeotia with a force of ten thousand troops. Near Leuctra, a village ten miles southwest of Thebes, the opposing phalanxes came to death grips. As planned, the formidable Theban left wing pushed back and eventually shattered the Spartan right. A thousand Spartans, including Cleombrotus, were killed, compared with a loss of only forty-seven Boeotians. The news of the event shocked Greeks everywhere. In a single afternoon, Epaminondas and his comrades had dispelled the myth of Spartan invincibility and made Thebes the dominant state of Greece.

## The Theban Hegemony

Sparta's humiliation at Leuctra significantly altered the political climate of Greece, especially in the Peloponnesus. Inspired and supported by Thebes, most of the Peloponnesian cities that had long been allied to Sparta out of fear terminated their Spartan-backed oligarchies and proclaimed independence. Democracy suddenly became the most prevalent political system in the area. At the same time, a confederacy similar to the Boeotian League was established in Arcadia, the central Peloponnesian region. Aided by Epaminondas, the Arcadians founded a new capital and named it Megalopolis, meaning "great city."

# The Spartans Routed at Leuctra

*This brief account of the battle in which Thebes destroyed the myth of Spartan invincibility was penned by the first-century B.C. Greek historian Diodorus Siculus in his* Library of History *(volume 7).*

When the trumpets on both sides sounded the charge and the armies simultaneously with the first onset raised the battle cry . . . they met in hand-to-hand combat, [and] at first both fought ardently and the battle was evenly poised; shortly, however, as Epaminondas's men began to derive advantage from . . . the denseness of their lines [i.e., larger-than-normal number of ranks of hoplites], many Peloponnesians began to fall. For they were unable to endure the weight of the courageous fighting of the elite corps [Thebes's Sacred Band]. . . . The Spartans were with great difficulty forced back; at first, as they gave ground they would not break their formation, but finally, as many fell and the commander who would have rallied them [Cleombrotus] had died, the army turned and fled in utter rout.

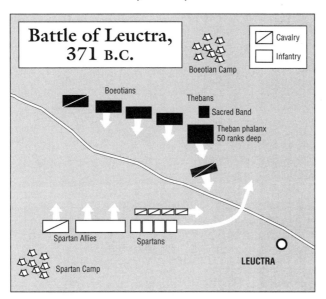

This was only the beginning of a series of bold actions taken by Epaminondas, whom many Greeks had come to see as a liberator. With a force of more than thirty thousand soldiers, he entered the Spartan home region of Laconia and, as Paul Cartledge says, came "close enough for the fires of burning crops and buildings to be seen and smelled by the inhabitants of unwalled Sparta."[48] The plan seems to have been not to attack the Spartan towns but merely to intimidate and humiliate the residents by demonstrating that such an assault *could* be launched if Thebes deemed it necessary.

After a few weeks, Epaminondas moved westward into Messenia, where thousands of Helots, who had recently rebelled once

*A surviving section of New Messene's walls reveals how formidable they were.*

Trying to maintain the new balance of power, the Boeotians under Epaminondas entered the Peloponnesus three more times in the years that followed. During this period, however, Theban leaders found that it was nearly impossible to maintain political stability in Greece without resorting to force from time to time. And inevitably, Thebes irritated or alienated a number of states, including some of its allies. Athens came to view the Theban hegemony with hostility, for example, and relations between the Arcadians and Thebans became increasingly strained.

In 362 B.C. Thebes sent an army into the Peloponnesus for the last time. Open warfare had recently broken out between some of the Arcadian cities and nearby Elis (which hosted the Olympic Games). Also, tensions among the central Peloponnesian states had escalated and Sparta had once again decided to flex its muscles and interfere in its neighbors' affairs. Epaminondas and his troops reached Mantinea (north of Megalopolis) in late summer and found themselves up against a powerful coalition of hoplites from Sparta, Athens, Elis, and various Arcadian cities.

The battle that ensued was the largest ever fought by Greeks against Greeks up to that time, involving more than fifty thousand men in all. Epaminondas arrayed his phalanx the same way he had at Leuctra. And his soldiers enjoyed considerable success, although not as much as before because this time his opponents had anticipated his tactics. The outcome was therefore indecisive. As Xenophon put it in his

more, were gathering. The Boeotians stayed long enough to ensure that Sparta did not interfere in the ongoing liberation. And they helped the freed Messenians establish a city of their own—New Messene, which featured massive stone walls, some of which still stand. As Epaminondas expected, the loss of Messenia was a devastating blow to Sparta, which had heavily relied on the grain it had received from the region.

history of the early fourth century B.C., the *Hellenica:*

> Both sides claimed the victory, but it cannot be said that with regard to the accession of new territory, or cities, or power either side was any better off after the battle than before it. In fact, there was even more uncertainty and confusion in Greece after the battle than there had been previously. [49]

## The Rise of Macedonia

Only three years after the bloody affair at Mantinea, an event occurred far to the north that most of the inhabitants of the city-states took little notice of. Perdiccas, king of Macedonia, was killed fighting the Illyrians, a neighboring hill people. That left his son, Philip II, then about twenty-two years old, as the new Macedonian monarch. One reason the city-state Greeks cared little about these events was that Macedonia lay on what they viewed as the distant fringes of their world. Also, Macedonia had long lain outside of Greece's cultural mainstream and appeared to most Greeks to be primitive and corrupt. The Athenians, Thebans, and their neighbors, in Peter Green's words,

> regarded Macedonians in general as semi-savages, uncouth of speech and dialect, retrograde in their political institutions, negligible as fighters, and habitual oath-breakers, who dressed in bear pelts and were much given to . . . [drunkenness], tempered with regular bouts of assassination and incest. [50]

This unflattering portrait was in many ways accurate (if somewhat exaggerated) before the shrewd, enterprising, and supremely ambitious Philip ascended the throne. Wasting no time, Philip secured Macedonia's borders. Then, with astonishing speed, he unified the inhabitants of the country's lowland and mountainous regions, who traditionally did not get along. One way Philip managed this task was by creating Europe's first national, professional standing army. Unlike the part-time militia of the city-states, his army was a permanent force whose members received extensive training. He also rewarded them with plots of farmland and

*A member of the King's Companions, Philip's elite force of mounted fighters.*

loot acquired in their conquests. These incentives motivated thousands of young men from all over Macedonia to join Philip's new national organization.

Philip also developed a new military system that integrated several different elements that supported and strengthened one another. One of these elements was a cavalry force (called the King's Companions) that was trained to make frontal assaults on enemy infantry. (Prior to this, horsemen were used mainly to guard the infantry's flanks, to try to outflank enemy infantry, or to chase down fleeing enemy soldiers.) Another element of Philip's new army was a more lethal version of the phalanx, which became known as the "Macedonian phalanx." First, Philip deepened the ranks of the traditional phalanx (as Epaminondas had done). Then he armed his soldiers with two-handed pikes ranging from twelve to eighteen feet long. Many of these projected from the front of the formation, creating an impenetrable and frightening mass of spearheads.

In addition to these military reforms, Philip introduced into Western warfare a new philosophy and goal of battle—naked conquest. Under his influence, Victor Hanson writes, warfare became

> much more than personal courage, nerve, and physical strength. Nor was killing by Macedonians just over territorial borders. Rather, the strategy of battle was designed predominantly as an instrument of ambitious state policy. . . . Philip's territorial ambitions had

nothing to do with a few acres outside the city-state, but rather encompassed a broader vision of mines, harbors, and tribute-paying communities that might be his solely to fuel his rapacious [victory-hungry] army. [51]

Philip's new military system began to prove itself in the years that followed. In 357 B.C. he captured Amphipolis, a former Athenian colony located about seventy miles east of the Macedonian capital of Pella. Although the Athenians declared war, they did not follow up, mainly because they lacked the will to send troops so far from home. This allowed Philip to grab the valuable gold and silver mines located north of Amphipolis, which helped finance his subsequent campaigns.

These and subsequent military expeditions gained Philip increasing amounts of territory and carried him closer and closer to his ultimate goal—Athens, Thebes, Corinth, and the other major city-states of southern Greece. For various reasons, most of these states did not take him very seriously at first. Indeed, for several years only one leading public figure consistently called attention to the threat Philip posed. That figure, the Athenian orator Demosthenes, delivered the first of his "Philippics," speeches denouncing Philip's conquests, in 351 B.C. Demosthenes said:

> Observe, Athenians, the height to which the fellow's insolence has soared. He leaves you no choice of action or inaction. . . . He cannot rest content

*A lethal mass of spear points projected from the front of Philip's phalanx. No enemy army that faced it head-on could withstand its charge.*

with what he has conquered; he is always taking in more, everywhere casting his net around us, while we sit idle and do nothing. When, Athenians, will you take the necessary action? What are you waiting for? [52]

## The Bloody Field of Chaeronea

To their later regret, the southern city-states did not heed Demosthenes' warnings until it was too late. In 346 B.C., Isocrates, now an old man, published an address in which he called on Philip to lead the Greek states in a war against Persia. Many Greeks were

dismayed, feeling that the orator's words would only flatter Philip and give him more reason to seek supremacy in Greece. They were right. That same year, Philip entered southern Greece and took control of the religious sanctuary at Delphi. "The news stunned the Athenians," Plutarch wrote in his biography of Demosthenes. "No speaker dared to mount the rostrum, nobody knew what advice should be given, the Assembly was struck dumb and appeared to be completely at a loss." [53]

At this point, it appears that Philip would have preferred to gain mastery over Athens and its neighbors through diplomacy, at least his version, which included veiled intimidation, half-truths, and sometimes outright lies. In large degree this was because he wanted them to accept him as a fellow Greek. He deeply admired Greek culture, fancied himself its champion, and desired to avoid despoiling the splendid

*Demosthenes, the Athenian orator who helped to organize resistance against Philip.*

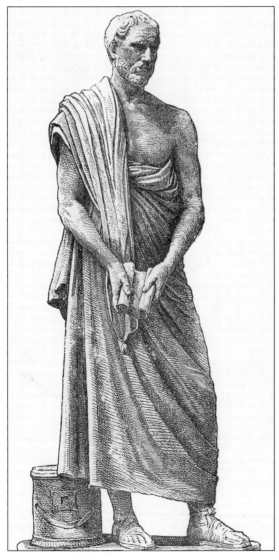

monuments of the southern cities. Philip was especially impressed by Athenian history and culture for some of the same reasons that people are today. Peter Green points out:

> The charismatic mystique [compelling romantic image] of the city that had broken the [Persian] king's ambitions at Marathon and Salamis, that had produced Aeschylus and Pericles and Plato, could not fail to leave its mark on him. His contempt was always mingled with a kind of wide-eyed colonial admiration. [54]

However, the Athenians and other southern Greeks viewed Philip as nothing more than a brutish, boorish interloper and decided to resist. His chief nemesis in the region, Demosthenes, rose to the occasion and almost single-handedly forged an anti-Macedonian alliance led by Athens and Thebes. The inevitable showdown took place in August 338 B.C. near Chaeronea, in western Boeotia. Aided by his eighteen-year-old son, Alexander III, who led the cavalry charge, Philip employed his new phalanx with devastating effect. The Athenians broke ranks and fled, followed by many others. The only allied contingent that stood its ground was Thebes's Sacred Band, whose members died fighting to the last man, like the Spartans at Thermopylae.

After his victory on the bloody field of Chaeronea, Philip forced the city-states to form a confederacy headed by himself. (Sparta was the only state that dared to

*This huge stone lion stands on the field of Chaeronea, a monument to the fallen.*

the invasion of 480 B.C. and other acts of aggression against the Greeks. To achieve those ends, the council of the alliance was empowered to pass decrees binding on member states, [and] to arbitrate disputes between them. . . . Member states . . . also received pledges of mutual nonaggression and promises of support against attack or subversion of their governments. Not surprisingly, Philip . . . was appointed *hegemon* ("leader") of the alliance and commander of the war of revenge against the Persians. [55]

Although few Greeks were happy about being forced to bow to Philip, there was little or nothing they could do to stop him. So in the wake of Macedonia's eclipse of the city-states, they began preparing to follow him into Asia. It was not Philip who ended up leading the fateful Persian campaign, however, as he was suddenly assassinated by a disgruntled Macedonian in 336 B.C. The immediate reactions in Athens and most other Greek states were relief and elation; the common view was that, without Philip, the Macedonian hegemony would collapse. Clearly, no one yet appreciated the talent, determination, and sheer brutality of his young successor, Alexander.

refuse to join.) "The purpose of the alliance was twofold," Sarah Pomeroy and her colleagues explain,

> to maintain a common peace in Greece and to retaliate against the Persians for

Chapter

# 6

# Alexander the Great: The Second Defeat of Persia

T he aged orator Isocrates died in 338 B.C., shortly after Philip's triumph at Chaeronea, and did not live to see the inauguration of the anti-Persian crusade he had so long advocated. Isocrates did not realize that Philip would soon be dead, nor could he have foreseen that the Macedonian crown prince Alexander, a young man barely out of his teens, would end up leading the fateful expedition. In fact, Alexander's youth and apparent lack of political experience at first caused many Greeks to underestimate his abilities and resolution. But he wasted little time in demonstrating both. Soon after Alexander took power, Thebes rebelled against Macedonian authority and Alexander swiftly and harshly punished the city. After some six thousand of the inhabitants had

been butchered in the streets, he sold the remaining thirty thousand into slavery and ordered nearly every building leveled.

In the wake of Thebes's demise, no other Greek state dared to defy Alexander. And this allowed him to proceed with his preparations for the march into Asia. He could not have anticipated at this early juncture that he would conquer all the lands stretching from Greece to India in only a decade and would create immense new political, economic, and social horizons for Greek civilization. Yet Alexander seemingly never doubted that he was destined somehow to change the world. He was obsessed with the idea that certain special humans are fated to achieve great deeds and everlasting fame. And he came to see himself as a later-day Achilles (the main hero of Homer's *Iliad*), who, it was said, chose a brief life of glory over a long one of obscurity. The second-century A.D. Greek historian Arrian, whose *Anabasis of Alexander* is the principal surviving source about Alexander's campaigns, recorded that Alexander told his soldiers: "Those who endure hardship and danger are the ones who achieve glory; and the most gratifying thing is to live with courage and to die leaving behind eternal renown." [56]

Alexander's phenomenal military successes assured him the immortality he desired. As for the reasons behind those successes, to begin with, he was an exceptionally gifted and bold military leader. He also had at his disposal the most formidable army the world had yet seen. "Alexander's greatest asset," says noted military historian J.F.C. Fuller, "was the army he inherited from his father; without it, in spite of his genius, his conquests would be

# What Did Alexander Look Like?

Although Alexander's exact physical features are unknown, scholars have a fairly good idea of what he looked like, partly because a number of busts of him have survived. These are not considered strictly realistic, because in ancient times sculptures of kings and heroes tended to glorify and ide-

*Macedonia's King Alexander, as shown in the Alexander Mosaic, unearthed in a house in Pompeii.*

alize their subjects to emphasize their supposed superiority to average people. Alexander is portrayed as ruggedly handsome, clean-shaven, with thick, flowing auburn hair. Perhaps the most intriguing artistic depiction of Alexander appears in a large mosaic scene found in the House of the Faun at Pompeii (the famous Roman town buried by a volcanic eruption in A.D. 79). Dubbed the "Alexander Mosaic" by scholars, it shows the climactic moment of a battle, probably the one fought at Issus in 333 B.C. Alexander is charging from the left-hand side of the picture toward King Darius, who stands in his chariot on the right side. The face of Alexander in this work may have been based on sculptures or paintings now lost.

inconceivable—it was an instrument exactly suited to his craft."[57]

No less important a factor in Alexander's success was his cold-bloodedness, which filled his enemies with fear and loathing. His wholesale destruction of Thebes, one of the oldest and most cultured cities in Greece, shocked Greeks everywhere. And even after the initial shock had worn off, as Peter Green puts it, "the attitude of the Greeks toward Alexander hardened into a bitter and implacable hatred."[58] Moreover, the brutality unleashed on the Thebans, Victor Hanson writes, proved

*Alexander leads his men across the Granicus and into the Persian ranks.*

simply a foretaste of the entire Alexandrian approach to military practice so successful later in Asia. [This approach included] the ultimatum of surrender, the preference of lethal force to negotiation, the subsequent obliteration of the enemy, the inevitable murder of women and children and razing of house and home . . . and always the dramatic and mythic flair to mask the barbarity, in the case of Thebes the sparing of the poet Pindar's house to emphasize [Alexander's] Greekness.[59]

These grim realities belie the old and now discarded view of Alexander as a romantic adventurer and reformer trying to unite the peoples of the known world, for their own good, into a sort of universal brotherhood.

## Victory at Granicus and Issus

However one sees Alexander's personality and intentions, his conquest of a large portion of western Asia ranks him as one of the pivotal figures of ancient times. His invasion of Persia began in April 334 B.C. when he led a force of thirty-two thousand infantry and five thousand cavalry across the Hellespont (now the Dardanelles) into Asia Minor. An army hastily thrown together by some local Persian governors soon confronted him at the Granicus River, east of the Hellespont. In Arrian's account, which was based on reliable sources, he described the opening moments of the contest:

There was a profound hush as both armies stood for a while motionless on

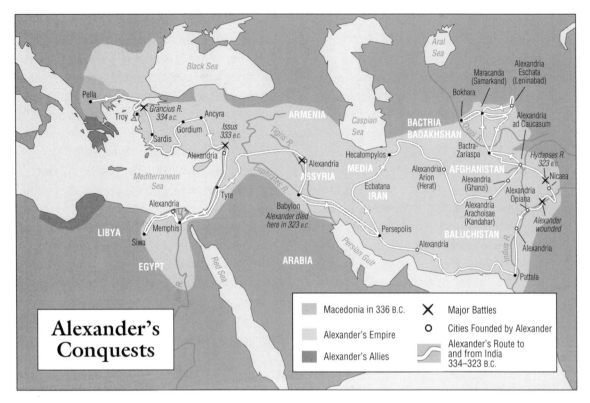

**Alexander's Conquests**

Legend:
- Macedonia in 336 B.C.
- Alexander's Empire
- Alexander's Allies
- ✕ Major Battles
- ○ Cities Founded by Alexander
- Alexander's Route to and from India 334–323 B.C.

Map labels: Aral Sea, Black Sea, Pella, Troy, Grancius R. 334 B.C., Ancyra, Gordium, Sardis, Issus 333 B.C., Alexandria, ARMENIA, Caspian Sea, Maracanda (Samarkand), Bokhara, Alexandria Eschata (Leninabad), Oxus R., BACTRIA BADAKHSHAN, Alexandria ad Caucasum, Bactra-Zariaspa, Hydaspes R. 323 B.C., Tigris R., Hecatompylos, MEDIA, Alexandria, ASSYRIA, Mediterranean Sea, Euphrates R., Alexandria, Tyre, Babylon Alexander died here in 323 B.C., Ecbatana, IRAN, Alexandria Arion (Herat), AFGHANISTAN, Alexandria (Ghanzi), Alexandria Opiana, Nicaea, Alexander wounded, Alexandria Arachoisae (Kandahar), Indus R., Persepolis, BALUCHISTAN, Alexandria, Alexandria, Pattala, LIBYA, Memphis, Siwa, Nile R., Red Sea, Persian Gulf, EGYPT, ARABIA

the brink of the river, as if in awe of what was to come. Then Alexander . . . at the head of the right wing of the army, with trumpets blaring . . . moved forward into the river. . . . The leading files [of his army] . . . were met as they gained the river bank by volleys of missiles from the Persians, who kept up a continuous fire into the river both from their commanding position on the high ground above, and also from the comparatively flat strip right down by the water's edge. A hand-to-hand struggle developed, the Greek mounted troops trying to force their way out of the water, the Persians doing their utmost to prevent them. Persian lances flew thick and fast, the long Greek spears thrust and stabbed. . . . Horse against horse, man against man, locked together, the Greeks did their utmost to thrust the enemy . . . back from the river bank . . . while the Persians fought to . . . hurl their opponents back into the water.

The Persian soldiers could not stop the onslaught of the Macedonian phalanx, however. Soon, Arrian continued, Alexander's opponents "were in a bad way. There was no escape for horse or rider from the thrust of the Macedonian spears. . . . Once the [Persians'] center had failed to hold, both wings of [their] cavalry broke, too, and the rout was complete." [60]

After his first major victory, Alexander marched southward into northwestern Syria, where the Persian king, Darius III, was waiting with a large army. In November 333 B.C., at Issus, near the Mediterranean coast, the two armies clashed. At first, the Persians put up stiff resistance, but Alexander's cavalry soon broke up and eliminated the enemy's left wing. And when the other Persians realized what had happened, most panicked and took flight, Darius himself among them. "The moment the Persian left went to pieces," Arrian recalled,

and Darius, in his war-chariot, saw that it was cut off, he . . . fled—indeed, he led the race for safety. Keeping to his chariot as long as there was smooth ground to travel on, he . . . [eventually abandoned it], leapt on a horse, and rode for his life. Darkness soon closed in; and that alone saved him from falling into the hands of Alexander. . . . Darius's headquarters were stormed and captured; his mother was taken, together with his wife . . . his infant son . . . [and] two of his daughters. [61]

## "Everything You Possess Is Now Mine"

Not long after the battle of Issus—in which the Greeks suffered 450 killed and 4,000 wounded, compared with 15,000 Persians killed, wounded, or captured—Alexander and Darius exchanged letters. Arrian preserved their substance, which included these words by Darius:

Since [my] reign began, Alexander has sent no representative to [my] court to confirm the former friendship and alliance between the two kingdoms; on the contrary, he has crossed into Asia with his armed forces and done much damage to the Persians. For this reason [I] took the field in defense of [my] country and of [my] ancestral throne. . . . The issue of the battle was as some god willed. And now Darius the King asks Alexander the King to restore from captivity his wife, his mother, and his children, and is willing to make friends with him and be his ally. For this cause [I] urge Alexander to send to [me] . . . representatives of his own in order that proper guarantees may be exchanged.

Alexander's response read in part:

Your ancestors invaded Macedonia and Greece and caused havoc in our country, though we had done nothing to provoke them. As supreme commander of all Greece I invaded Asia because I wished to punish Persia for this act, an act which must be laid wholly to your charge. . . . First I defeated in battle your generals and [governors]; now I have defeated yourself and the army you led. By God's help I am master of your country, and I have made myself responsible for the survivors of your army who fled to me for refuge. Far from being detained by force, they are serving of their own free will under my command. Come to me, therefore, as you would come to the lord of the continent of Asia. . . . And in the future let any communication you wish to make with me be addressed to the King of all Asia. Do not write to me as an equal. Everything you possess is now mine; so if you should want anything, let me know in the proper terms . . . or I shall take steps to deal with you as a criminal. If, on the other hand, you wish to dispute your throne, stand and fight for it and do not run away. Wherever you may hide yourself, be sure I shall seek you out.[62]

As the heir to a long line of absolute monarchs over a vast empire, Darius no doubt viewed these words as insolent and arrogant and had no intention of assuming a subservient position. Still, he badly wanted to get his family back. Also, he must have recognized that Alexander was a dangerous adversary who might inflict further damage on the Persian realm. For these reasons, Darius later sent Alexander an unusually generous offer, which Arrian summarized as follows:

[Darius] offered a sum of 10,000 talents [the equivalent of many millions of dollars today] in exchange for his mother, wife, and children . . . [and] proposed that all the [Near Eastern] territory west of the Euphrates [River]

*Alexander greets Darius's mother, wife, and children, whom the Greeks captured at Issus. Alexander ordered that they be treated well.*

. . . should belong to Alexander, who should seal his bond of friendship and alliance with Persia by marrying Darius's daughter. . . . [Alexander's top general Parmenio] declared that were he Alexander he would be happy to end the war on such terms and be done with any further adventures. "That," replied Alexander, "is what I should do if I were Parmenio. But since I am Alexander, I shall send Darius a different answer."

That answer was that Alexander had no need of a portion of the Persian realm, since he already owned all of it, and that if he wanted to marry the princess, he would do so whether Darius liked it or not. "Upon receiving this reply," Arrian wrote, "Darius abandoned all thought of coming to terms and began to prepare once more for war."[63]

## The Slaughter at Tyre and Gaza

Between communications with Darius, Alexander was not idle, but continued southward into Palestine. His purpose, as military historians Nicholas Sekunda and John Warry point out, "was to leave no possible Persian base in his rear before marching eastward to resume hostilities with Darius himself."[64]

Among these bases were the Phoenician cities along the coast. Most submitted to Alexander without a fight, but the highly fortified island-city of Tyre was defiant. The Tyrians managed to hold out against a fearsome siege for seven months (January to July

332 B.C.) but finally succumbed after the attackers constructed a massive earthen causeway from the mainland to the island. Entering the city, Alexander's soldiers slew more than six thousand people in the streets, then crucified more than two thousand men and sold perhaps as many as thirty thousand women and children into slavery. Farther south, another coastal city—Gaza—also made the

*Alexander directs the siege of Tyre, which fell after seven months.*

# Conceiving Alexandria's Layout

*When Alexander decided to build the new city of Alexandria in Egypt, he chose the architect Deinocrates, of the Greek island city-state of Rhodes, to design it. However, a number of modern scholars agree that the king himself personally conceived the city's general layout. In his biography of Alexander, Plutarch included this fascinating anecdote (translated by Ian Scott-Kilvert in* The Age of Alexander *) concerning an omen that supposedly occurred at the time.*

There was no chalk to mark the ground plan. So they took barley meal, sprinkled it on the dark earth, and marked out a semi-circle, which was divided into equal segments by lines radiating from the inner arc to the circumference. . . . While the king was enjoying the symmetry of the design, suddenly huge flocks of birds appeared from the river and the lagoon, descended upon the site, and devoured every grain of the barley. Alexander was greatly disturbed by this omen, but the diviners [those in charge of interpreting omens] urged him to take heart and interpreted the occurrence as a sign that the city would not only have abundant resources of its own, but would be the nurse of men of innumerable nations, and so he ordered those in charge of the work to proceed.

*A sketch shows some of the buildings bordering Alexandria's harbor. Alexander died well before the city's completion.*

mistake of resisting. The price it paid was the slaughter of all its men and the sale and servitude of all its women and children. At Alexander's order, the city's governor was bound, had his ankles attached to the back of a chariot, and was dragged to death.

The following December, Alexander entered and took charge of one of Darius's most important eastern bases, Egypt, which had been under Persian rule off and on for two centuries. The acquisition of one of the world's most ancient, venerable, and grain-rich lands was a welcome addition to the Macedonian king's growing empire. But Alexander was disappointed when he reached Egypt's ancient capital of Memphis. In his mind, the city was not a suitable capital because it was situated too far (ninety miles) from the sea. Reasoning that Egypt's resources could be best exploited through a major Mediterranean port, Alexander determined that he would build a new capital for Egypt in the Nile Delta. According to Plutarch, Alexander "had chosen a site on the advice of his architects," but then remembered a passage from Homer's *Odyssey* that mentioned an island in the Delta named Pharos that was supposedly ideal for launching ships. Brimming with enthusiasm, Alexander hurried to Pharos and

> when he saw what wonderful natural advantages the place possessed—for it was a strip of land resembling a broad isthmus which stretched between the sea and a great lagoon [Lake Mareotis], with a spacious harbor at the end of it— he declared that Homer, besides his

other admirable qualities, was also a far-seeing architect, and he ordered the plan of the city to be designed so that it would conform to this site. [65]

The new city, which the Macedonian king called Alexandria (one of many new cities he established and named after himself), went on to become one of the leading metropolises of the known world. However, its founder never saw it completed. In July 331 B.C., only seven months after entering Egypt, Alexander led his forces toward the northeast for the long-anticipated assault on Persia's heartland (now occupied by Iraq and southern Iran).

## Darius's Last Stand and Gallant Death

On October 1, Alexander's army, which now numbered some forty thousand infantry and seven thousand cavalry, reached Gaugamela (meaning "the camel's house"), about 270 miles north of Babylon. There, Darius made his last stand at the head of a host of one hundred thousand or more troops, two hundred war chariots, and fifteen battle elephants. "With shouts of encouragement to one another," Plutarch wrote, the Macedonian cavalry "charged the enemy at full speed and the phalanx rolled forward like a flood." As the Persian ranks began to fall back, Alexander caught sight of Darius and rushed directly at him. At this, Darius's bodyguards

> were seized with panic at the terrible sight of Alexander bearing down upon them . . . and the greater number of

*Alexander kneels over the dead body of Darius. With Darius's death, the Persian royal line and the empire it ruled came to an end.*

them broke and scattered. . . . As for Darius, all the horrors of the battle were now before his eyes. . . . He abandoned his chariot and his armor, mounted a mare . . . and rode away. [66]

Following Alexander's overwhelming victory, in which more than fifty thousand Persians were killed (compared with fewer than a thousand Greeks), some of his soldiers pursued Darius for many miles. But once more the Persian monarch managed to elude them. While these soldiers continued the search, Alexander moved unopposed into the Persian homeland of Fars, where he put the splendid capital of Persepolis to the torch. Alexander also occupied the other two Persian capitals—Babylon and Susa, neither of which offered any resistance.

It was not long before Alexander learned that Bessus, governor of the Persian province of Bactria, and other high Persian officials had captured King Darius. Bessus had declared himself the new Persian king. And he and his compatriots were prepared to exchange their prisoner for what Arrian called "favorable terms for themselves." Hearing this, Alexander gathered some trusted men and "pressed his pursuit" of the fugitives "without a moment's delay." [67] When Bessus and the other conspirators realized that the Greeks were rapidly closing in on them, they panicked, stabbed Darius with their spears, and fled.

Less than an hour later, one of Alexander's forward scouts, a man named Polystratus, came upon a driverless covered wagon near a stream and heard faint groans from within. He found Darius, bound and bleeding and accompanied only by his faithful dog. The wounded man asked for water and Polystratus obliged. Then Darius mustered what strength he could and said feebly:

> This is the final stroke of misfortune, that I should accept a service from you, and not be able to return it, but Alexander will reward you for your kindness, and the gods will repay him for his courtesy towards my mother and my wife and my children. And so through you, I give him my hand. [68]

With these gallant words, the last Persian ruler passed, along with his empire, into history.

When Alexander arrived soon afterward, he was angry that he had been robbed of meeting and dealing with Darius himself. After the Macedonian king caught up with Bessus, Plutarch wrote,

> he had the tops of two straight trees bent down so that they met, and part of Bessus's body was tied to each. Then, when each tree was let go and sprang back to its upright position, the part of

## Admiration for Alexander's Legend

*In the conclusion of his* Anabasis, *the Greek historian Arrian summed up Alexander's qualities. It must be kept in mind that Arrian lived more than four centuries after his subject died, so these words, along with Arrian's admiration for Alexander, were influenced to some degree by the latter's already highly romanticized legend.*

He had great personal beauty, invincible power of endurance, and a keen intellect. . . . He had an uncanny instinct for the right course in a difficult and complex situation. . . . Noble indeed was his power of inspiring his men, of filling them with confidence, and . . . sweeping away their fear by the spectacle of his own fearlessness. . . . There was in those days no nation, no city, no single individual beyond the reach of Alexander's name. Never in all the world was there another like him, and therefore I cannot but feel that some power more than human was concerned in his birth . . . and there is the further evidence of the extraordinary way in which he is held, as no mere man could be, in honor and remembrance. . . . In the course of this book I have, admittedly, found fault with some of the things which Alexander did, but of the man himself, I am not ashamed to express ungrudging admiration.

the body attached to it was torn off in the recoil. [69]

## To India and Back

In the years following Darius's defeat and death, Alexander continued into the eastern provinces of the former Persian realm (a region now encompassed by eastern Iran and Afghanistan). The Greeks subdued the locals everywhere they went and Alexander left garrisons of soldiers to hold various outposts. He also established more towns, the most distant of which was Alexandria Eschate ("Farthest Alexandria"), lying some twenty-four hundred miles from Greece.

Late in 327 B.C. Alexander and his men reached India and crossed the Indus River, where they were welcomed in the city of Taxila and received the submission of several Indian rulers who had heard of their deeds. One local king, Porus, was not so willing to cooperate, however, and rallied his army at the Hydaspes River in May 326 B.C. Alexander defeated Porus and may well have gone on to conquer the rest of India. But the Macedonian troops, exhausted from their seemingly endless trek and homesick besides, demanded that they be allowed to turn back. Alexander attempted to change their minds, to no avail. Arrian wrote:

> He at last submitted, and . . . made a public announcement that . . . he had decided upon withdrawal. . . . [Many of his soldiers] wept. They came to Alexander's tent and called down every blessing upon him for allowing them to prevail—the only defeat he had ever suffered. [70]

The return journey was long and difficult, and many of Alexander's men died along the way. He and the survivors reached Babylon in the spring of 323 B.C. Shortly afterward, on June 10, Alexander died, possibly of malaria. He was only thirty-three. The empire he had carved out in only a few years was the largest the world had yet seen. But ominously, he did not name an heir, and the burning question now became, which of Alexander's leading followers should administer his vast realm? No answer satisfactory to all could be found. The result was to be forty years of chaos and bloodshed, followed by the emergence of a new and in many ways very different Greek world.

# The Successor States and Greece's Decline

In the decades following the passing of Alexander, who became known as "the Great," the Near East received an influx of hundreds of thousands of Greek soldiers, city planners, administrators, merchants, and artisans. They spread their language, ideas, and culture over an area dozens of times larger than mainland Greece. And in the process, the former Persian realm was transformed at a pace that many who remembered the days of Philip, Demosthenes, and Darius found disconcerting. One of these elders was an Athenian statesman named Demetrius of Phaleron, who asked:

Can you imagine that fifty years ago if some god had foretold the future to the Persians or their king, or the Macedonians or their king, they would have believed that the very name of the Persians would now be lost, who at one time were masters of almost the whole inhabited world, while the Macedonians, whose name was formerly unknown, would now be masters of it all? Nevertheless, Fortune . . . causes events to happen in defiance of our expectations.[71]

Equally surprising to many was that the huge empire Alexander had carved out barely outlived him. Almost immediately, his leading generals and governors began to bicker, and in time these former comrades in arms resorted to violence. For roughly forty years, the wars waged by these men, who came to be called the *Diadochoi* ("Successors"), caused widespread death, destruction, chaos, and fear. Meanwhile, one by one, the Successors eliminated one another.

Finally, by about 280 B.C., a handful of the combatants emerged victorious and looked out over a dramatically altered political landscape. The eastern Mediterranean and Near Eastern spheres were now dominated by a few large so-called successor states. One was the Macedonian Kingdom, made up mostly of Macedonia and portions of the Greek mainland. Another, the Seleucid Kingdom, founded by one of Alexander's generals, Seleucus, covered most of what are now Iraq, Iran, and Turkey. And a third, the Ptolemaic Kingdom, established by another of the Successors, Ptolemy, encompassed Egypt and parts of nearby Palestine. The smaller states included the kingdoms of Pergamum (in western Asia Minor) and Epirus (in northwestern Greece); the Aetolian League (in western Greece) and Achaean League (in the Peloponnesus), federations of cities that had banded together for mutual protection; and some strong independent city-states, notably Athens, the Aegean island of Rhodes, and Byzantium (near the entrance to the Black Sea).

Modern scholars call these realms, as they existed in the post-Alexander era, Hellenistic,

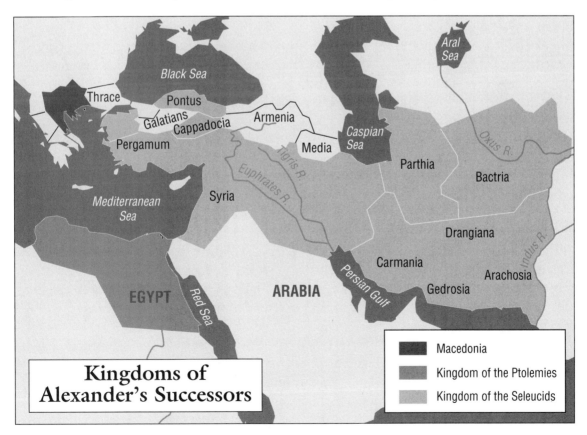

**Kingdoms of Alexander's Successors**

Legend:
- Macedonia
- Kingdom of the Ptolemies
- Kingdom of the Seleucids

meaning "Greek-like." This is because many of their societies featured various Eastern languages, customs, and ideas overlaid by a coating of Greek ones. Similarly, the historical period beginning with Alexander's death in 323 B.C. and ending with the demise of the last Hellenistic ruler (Cleopatra VII) in 30 B.C. is known as the Hellenistic Age.

On the whole, the Hellenistic realms demonstrated the same faults as earlier Greek states—disunity, rivalry, and nearly relentless warfare. But there was a glimmer of hope for the future of Greek civilization. Though they, too, often squabbled with their neighbors, the Aetolian and Achaean leagues were earnest and significant experiments in lasting unity among the old-style Greek city-states. Any hopes for the emergence of a "United States of Greece" were dashed, however, by the intrusion of the Romans, masters of the Italian peninsula, into the eastern Mediterranean starting in the early second century B.C. Rome eventually defeated and absorbed the Greeks, bringing their long dominance of Western civilization to a close.

## The Inhabited World

Although the Hellenistic Greeks largely lacked political unity, they shared many aspects of Greek culture. The widespread dissemination of Greek language, customs, and ideas in the eastern Mediterranean and Near East in these years created a huge cultural sphere. People came to call it the *oikoumene* (ee-koo-MEH-nee), or "inhabited world." A person could travel from one end of the Hellenistic sphere to the other and

feel more or less at home almost anywhere within it.

However, feeling at home is not the same as feeling that one is treated well and fairly. Hellenistic society was highly class oriented, with Greeks occupying the social upper crust. This is not surprising considering that Greeks founded and controlled virtually all the states in the *oikoumene*. Greek Koine (a form of Greek that developed from the Athenian dialect) became the universal language of administration and business, and those who could not speak, read, and write it were at a severe disadvantage. "In all instances," Peter Green says in his massive study of the Hellenistic world,

> what the Successors set up were enclaves of Greco-Macedonian culture in an alien world, governmental ghettos for a ruling elite. [With all the] Greek temples, Greek theaters, Greek gymnasia, Greek mosaics, and Greek-language inscriptions scattered through the *oikoumene*, we should never forget that it was for the Hellenized Macedonian ruling minority and its Greek supporters . . . that such home-from-home luxuries . . . [were] provided. . . . The gymnasium resembled an exclusive club; entry was highly selective . . . designed to keep out undesirables (i.e., non-Greeks).[72]

As members of the privileged class in many parts of the inhabited world, Greeks enjoyed autonomy, economic opportunities, and leisure time that often stimulated notable achievements in science. Greek scientists, par-

# Pergamum: A Cultural Center

One of the smallest of the Hellenistic kingdoms was also the most culturally splendid. Pergamum (or Pergamon), located in western Asia Minor, was at first a part of the Seleucid realm. But about 262 B.C. it broke away under the leadership of Philetaerus and his adopted son Eumenes, who founded the Attalid dynasty (named after Philetaerus's father, the Macedonian Attalus). Under the Attalids, Pergamum often dominated affairs in Asia Minor and became a renowned cultural center, with the second-largest library in the world (next to the one in the Ptolemaic city of Alexandria). Hellenistic architecture and sculpture also reached their height in the Great Altar of Zeus, erected

by the Attalid ruler Eumenes II in the second century B.C. The altar consisted of a grand staircase topped by a massive and stately colonnaded podium. Around the podium ran a magnificent sculpted panel showing Zeus and Athena doing battle with an army of giants; the sculptors captured the sweeping movement, drama, horror, and anguish of the scene with amazing skill.

*The Great Altar of Zeus at Pergamum as it likely appeared in its heyday.*

ticularly those working in Alexandria, which had become the known world's foremost commercial and intellectual center, made significant strides in anatomy, astronomy, and other fields. This spirit of searching for the underlying truth of things found further expression in the arts, as poets, sculptors, and painters achieved levels of vividness and realism unknown in prior ages. Michael

Grant points out that the vibrant new spirit of the age also stimulated an increased fascination for

the individual human being and his mind and emotions, an interest given vigorous expression by biographers and portrait artists. And this concern for the individual was extended not only

*This scale model shows the acropolis at Pergamum, with its series of terraces leading to the rulers' palaces at the top.*

to men but to women, whose position in society, literature, and art underwent an unprecedented transformation that was one of the most remarkable evolutionary changes of the age.[73]

Architecture also flourished in a renaissance nearly as resplendent as the one that had produced the Parthenon and its sister temples in the fifth century B.C. According to Graham Shipley, a noted authority on the Hellenistic Greeks:

The civic architecture and monuments of the Hellenistic period are often easy to distinguish from earlier and later buildings; different architectural orders are inventively combined, and there is a general impression of grandeur. . . . The third-century [B.C.] rulers of Pergamum [produced the most impressive example by exploiting] the steep terrain of the

city's acropolis to best effect. . . . The public buildings were grouped . . . on different terraces mounting up the acropolis. Each terrace held an imposing group of monuments forming an architectural unity. . . . On the highest part of the acropolis were a grand sanctuary of Athena, a theater, the library [the second largest in the known world], and the palaces of the kings.[74]

## Roman Troops on Greek Soil

Sadly, the Hellenistic Greeks devoted at least as much energy and effort to making war as they did to creating high culture, and that ultimately proved to be their undoing. The reasons for their discords were many and complex. Border disputes were common, especially between the Ptolemies and Seleucids over possession of Syria and Palestine. Another issue that frequently led to conflict was the need to control the communication and travel lines connecting mainland Greece and the Aegean region to various parts of the Near East. It was essential for the Seleucids and Ptolemies to maintain a steady flow of administrators, colonists, and artisans from Greece. Mercenary soldiers were even more crucial, since all of the Hellenistic rulers used them to supplement their standing armies drawn from the local citizenry. (The hired troops often received land grants in return for their military ser-

vice.) The Hellenistic monarchs also fought over access to the great trade routes that ran west to east through the Near East.

As time went on, history seemed to repeat itself, as the relentless disagreements and wars among the Hellenistic states weakened them and left them vulnerable to exploitation by an outside power. That power, Rome, became involved in the Greek sphere in the following manner. From 264 to 241 B.C. the Romans fought

# Hellenistic Sieges

Sieges had been an occasional feature of Greek warfare ever since the Bronze Age. But those involving siege towers, artillery, and other large-scale devices became common only after the mid–fourth century B.C., when Philip II proved their effectiveness in his sieges of various Greek cities. His son Alexander's sieges of Halicarnassus (334 B.C.) and Tyre (332 B.C.) subsequently became the models followed by the Hellenistic generals.

All of these leaders owed much to an earlier Greek military genius—Dionysius I, dictator and military commander of the powerful Sicilian Greek city of Syracuse. Dionysius offered hefty rewards to inventors to come up with new siege devices and by 397 B.C. was able to mount a devastating attack on the Carthaginian city of Motya. In the Syracusan arsenal were siege towers six stories high that moved on wheels and hundreds of mechanical crossbows. The well-fortified towers provided cover for men operating large battering rams. Once these rams smashed their way in, Dionysius ordered the towers into the town and dropped wooden gangways onto the rooftops; his troops then poured out of the towers and took control of the buildings.

These devices and tactics remained basic to Philip, Alexander, and the Successors, although their sieges did utilize other elements as well. One common element was mining (digging tunnels), which was done either to weaken and collapse a city's defensive walls or to transport troops beneath them. Greek inventors also introduced torsion-powered catapults, which propelled large bolts or stones up to half a mile or more.

and defeated the maritime empire of Carthage (centered in Tunisia, in North Africa) in the destructive First Punic War. Soon afterward, in 218, the even more calamitous Second Punic War began. During this conflict, one of the leading Hellenistic kings, Macedonia's Philip V, allied himself with Carthage, which earned him the enmity of Rome. In 202, shortly before the battle that ended the conflict in Rome's favor, Philip made another unwise move. He and the Seleucid ruler, Antiochus III, joined forces with the intention of attacking and dividing up the lands of Ptolemaic Egypt. Seeing this as a dangerous shift in the balance of power in the region, the leaders of Rhodes and Pergamum asked the Romans to intervene.

The Senate (then Rome's leading governmental branch) probably worried that an alliance between Macedonia and Seleucia might one day threaten Rome as well as the Greek lands. So the senators sent envoys to Philip to warn him that if he attacked any other Greek state he would find himself at odds with Rome. Reacting to what he saw as Roman insolence, Philip rejected this ultimatum. His defiance, combined with the memory of his earlier interference in the Second Punic War, motivated the Romans to declare war on him in 200 B.C.

Though not big or long as wars go, the Second Macedonian War (as the Romans called it) was important because it was the first time that Rome landed troops on Greek soil. The conflict was also significant because it showcased the first major confrontation between Europe's two most formidable and feared military systems. The mainstay of the Greek armies was still the Macedonian phalanx developed by Philip II. Though formidable, it operated as a single large unit and had little flexibility. In contrast, the Roman army featured many maniples, small units of soldiers that could move around the battlefield quickly, either singly or in groups. Polybius, who saw both military systems in action, wrote:

> The phalanx soldier cannot operate either in smaller units or singly, whereas the Roman formation is highly flexible. Every Roman soldier, once he is armed and goes into action, can adapt himself equally well to any place or time and meet an attack from any quarter. [75]

Philip learned about the qualities of the Roman army the hard way in the course of the final, decisive battle of the war. It took place in 197 B.C. at Cynoscephalae, a steep hill in central Greece. While the Roman commander Titus Quinctius Flamininus led a contingent of his troops against part of Philip's phalanx from the front, several maniples fighting on another section of the hill left their positions and fell on the rear of the formation. Most of the Macedonian soldiers could not swing their long pikes around in time to defend their backs, and large numbers of them were slain. People across the Greek world were stunned when they learned Philip had lost eight thousand dead and five thousand captured, while only seven hundred Romans had been killed.

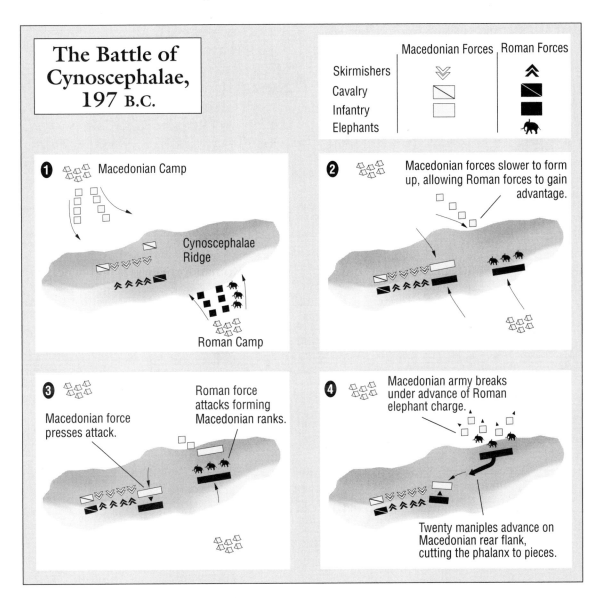

The Battle of
Cynoscephalae,
197 B.C.

| | Macedonian Forces | Roman Forces |
|---|---|---|
| Skirmishers | | |
| Cavalry | | |
| Infantry | | |
| Elephants | | |

**1** Macedonian Camp

Cynoscephalae Ridge

Roman Camp

**2** Macedonian forces slower to form up, allowing Roman forces to gain advantage.

**3** Macedonian force presses attack.

Roman force attacks forming Macedonian ranks.

**4** Macedonian army breaks under advance of Roman elephant charge.

Twenty maniples advance on Macedonian rear flank, cutting the phalanx to pieces.

# Catastrophe at Magnesia

Philip was so badly defeated, in fact, that he had no choice but to ask for surrender terms. Macedonia had to give up most of its warships, pay the Romans large sums of money, and promise to become Rome's ally. Clearly, the Romans now had a major foothold in Greece, which most Greeks feared would be used to launch operations against other Hellenistic states sooner or later. Moreover, the Romans wanted something in return for liberating a number of Greek cities that had formerly been unwilling subjects of Macedonia. Rome expected that in the future these cities would pursue a foreign policy that benefited Roman interests.

Many Greeks viewed this as an intolerable intrusion into their affairs. Hoping to rid themselves of the Romans, some leading Greeks asked the Seleucid king, Antiochus, to cross the Aegean and deal with the intruders. Antiochus agreed to the request and landed an advance force of ten thousand men on the mainland in 192 B.C. This action proved to be a grave miscalculation, for a Roman general soon arrived with twenty thousand troops and drove the small Seleucid army to the pass of Thermopylae. Antiochus hoped to avoid getting trapped there, as Leonidas and his Spartans had three centuries before. So he had two thousand of his Greek allies guard the infamous mountain path. A contingent of Roman soldiers dislodged these troops, however, which allowed a flanking movement exactly like that of the Persians against Leonidas. Seeing the Romans bearing down on their rear, Antiochus's men panicked, cast away their weapons, and fled.

The Romans were not finished with Antiochus. In 190 B.C., they landed an army

## A Greek Pleads for His People to Unite

*In 213 B.C. a Greek orator, Agelaus of Aetolia, recognized the potential danger that Rome's rising power posed to the Greeks and delivered the following prophetic warning, which was preserved by the second-century B.C. Greek historian Polybius in his* Histories. *Unfortunately for Greece, Agelaus's words were largely ignored.*

It would be best of all if the Greeks never went to war with one another, if they could regard it as the greatest gift of the gods for them to speak with one voice, and could join hands like men who are crossing a river; in this way they could unite to repulse the incursions of the barbarians and to preserve themselves and their cities. But if we have no hope of achieving such a degree of unity for the whole of the country, let me impress on you how important it is at least for the present that we should consult one another and remain on our guard, in view of the huge armies which have been mobilized, and vast scale of the war [the Second Punic War] which is now being waged in the west. For it must already be obvious to all those who pay even the slightest attention to affairs of state that whether the Carthaginians defeat the Romans or the Romans the Carthaginians, the victors will by no means be satisfied with the sovereignty of Italy and Sicily, but will come here, and will advance both their forces and their ambitions beyond the bounds of justice.

of thirty thousand, which included a few Greek allies from the Achaean League, on the coast of Ionia. At Magnesia, a few miles inland from the Aegean coast, this force faced off with a Seleucid army more than twice its size. Antiochus himself "was on the right flank" of his host, the first-century B.C. Roman historian Livy reported. No doubt the king was confident that his superior numbers would bring him victory. But a chain reaction of events soon made the Seleucid army collapse like a house of cards. The Achaeans showered the Seleucid chariots with javelins and rocks, causing them to retreat in fear and confusion. Seeing this, the Seleucid light-armed troops that were supposed to support the phalanx "were terrified," Livy wrote, and "also turned and fled." These men, in turn, caused Antiochus's horsemen to panic. At this point, "the whole left flank" of the Seleucid army "gave ground" and the panic spilled into the phalanx in the center. The king also joined in the flight. "Thus the Romans were victorious on both wings," said Livy, "and they made their way over piles of corpses which they had heaped up."[76]

For the Greeks in general, who were proud of their legacy of victories in many famous battles of the past, the affair at Magnesia was a major embarrassment. For Antiochus, it was an utter catastrophe. He lost an estimated 50,000 infantry and 3,000 cavalry, compared with only 350 Romans killed. Immediate surrender was his only viable option, and he took it. Antiochus was forced to turn over all but ten of his ships, to abandon control of western Asia Minor, and to pledge never again to attack Rome or its allies, a promise he kept.

## Rome's Hard Line Against Greece

By contrast, Philip V did not keep the similar promise he had given the Romans after they had defeated him a few years before. Bitter over that defeat, he slowly and quietly began rebuilding his nation's military resources. Philip died in 179 B.C. without getting his revenge, but his son, Perseus, who succeeded him, continued planning to fight the Romans. The Third Macedonian War (171–168 B.C.) soon erupted. And its climax, at Pydna (near Greece's northeastern coast), showed once more that the heyday of the phalanx was over. "The strength of the phalanx is irresistible when it is close-packed and bristling with extended spears," Livy wrote.

But if by attacks at different points you force the troops to swing round their spears, unwieldy as they are by reason of their length and weight, they become entangled in a disorderly mass. . . . That is what happened in this battle, when the phalanx was forced to meet the Romans who were attacking in small groups, with the Macedonian line broken at many points. The Romans kept infiltrating their files [ranks of soldiers] at every place where a gap offered. . . . For a long time the phalanx was cut to pieces from the front, the flanks, and the rear. In the end, those who slipped from the hands of the Romans . . . met

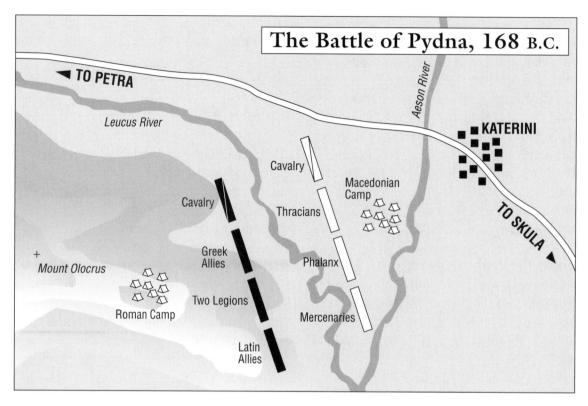

**The Battle of Pydna, 168 B.C.**

◀ TO PETRA

*Leucus River*

*Aeson River*

■ KATERINI

TO SKULA ▶

Cavalry

Thracians

Macedonian
Camp

Cavalry

Greek
Allies

Phalanx

+
*Mount Olocrus*

Two Legions

Roman Camp

Mercenaries

Latin
Allies

with destruction in a more horrible shape; for the [Macedonian] elephants [which by this time were in disarray] . . . trampled down the men . . . and crushed them to death.[77]

The casualty lists revealed the enormity of the Roman victory. Perseus lost twenty-five thousand men, while fewer than a hundred Romans were killed. He also lost his throne and suffered the humiliation of arrest and captivity in Rome, where he soon died. The Romans then dismantled the kingdom of Macedonia and replaced it with four smaller states that were expected thereafter to support Rome in all matters without question.

After that the Romans took a similar hard line with other Greeks, sometimes taking preemptive measures to forestall trouble. Roman troops rounded up more than a thousand prominent Achaean citizens (among them the historian Polybius) and kept them as hostages in Rome to make sure their cities behaved. Meanwhile, the Rhodians were compelled to give up their territories in Asia Minor, and in Epirus, the general who had defeated Perseus at Pydna destroyed seventy towns and sold 150,000 of their residents into slavery. The depredations against the Greeks continued. In the early 140s B.C., Rome abolished the four Macedonian republics it had recently created and annexed the region outright as a

Roman province. Then, in 146 B.C., a Roman general dissolved the Achaean League and demolished its capital, the once great city of Corinth.

## Into the Realm of Legend

By the end of the second century B.C., the Macedonian Kingdom and Epirus had been erased from the map and the Achaean and Aetolian leagues no longer existed. Meanwhile, the Seleucid realm was impotent and rapidly shrinking (at the hands of the Romans in the west and a central Asian people, the Parthians, in the east). The last of the former great Hellenistic kingdoms—Ptolemaic Egypt—had been spared for the moment. But it was by now a third-rate power whose Greek rulers were ineffectual or incompetent or both. They followed an unwritten rule that held that as long as they did Rome's bidding in the international scene, they would be allowed to remain independent and pursue their own local affairs.

This situation was not destined to last, however. Egypt possessed immense stores of grain and royal treasure, so it increasingly became a prize sought after by wealthy and power-hungry Romans. Cleopatra VII, last of the Ptolemies, reasoned that allying herself with such men might be good for both her and Egypt. And between 48 and 41 B.C., she allied herself, both politically and sexually, with two of the strongest Romans of the day—Julius Caesar (who was assassinated in 44 B.C.) and Mark Antony.

For a while, it appeared that Cleopatra and Antony might unite Rome's eastern provinces and much of the Near East into their own imperial domain and challenge Rome's western half for Mediterranean supremacy. However, a third Roman notable, the shrewd and ruthless Octavian (later Augustus Caesar, the first Roman emperor),

*A surviving statue depicts Cleopatra VII, last of the Ptolemaic and Hellenistic rulers, wearing an Egyptian headdress.*

opposed them. In 31 B.C. he delivered the lovers a decisive defeat in a sea battle at Actium (in western Greece). And the following year, Cleopatra and Antony took their own lives. In this way, the last major independent Greek ruler of the ancient world passed into the realm of legend, after which her kingdom became a Roman province.

In the decades and centuries that followed, the Greeks and their towns, still scattered across the Mediterranean world, existed within the framework of the Roman Empire. Prominent Greeks such as the writers Plutarch and Arrian became proud Roman citizens, soldiers, and officials; yet they took equal pride in their Greek roots and culture, which came to exert a profound influence on Roman civilization. Roman art, architecture, literature, religion, and much more owed an incalculable debt to Greece, and Greco-Roman culture later came to shape Western society and thought in innumerable ways. Thus, although the history of ancient Greece ended long ago, the spirit of that land and its remarkable people endures.

# Notes

## Introduction: Why Study the Greeks?

1. Sarah B. Pomeroy et al., *Ancient Greece: A Political, Social, and Cultural History.* New York: Oxford University Press, 1999, p. 14.
2. Chester G. Starr, *The Ancient Greeks.* New York: Oxford University Press, 1971, p. 4.
3. Charles Freeman, *The Greek Achievement: The Foundation of the Western World.* New York: Viking, 1999, p. 434.
4. Will Durant, *The Life of Greece.* New York: Simon and Schuster, 1966, pp. 670–71.

## Chapter 1: Greece in the Bronze and Dark Ages

5. Pomeroy et al., *Ancient Greece*, p. 6.
6. J.V. Luce, *Lost Atlantis: New Light on an Old Legend.* New York: McGraw-Hill, 1969, p. 183.
7. Thomas R. Martin, *Ancient Greece: From Prehistoric to Hellenistic Times.* New Haven, CT: Yale University Press, 1996, p. 27.
8. Carol G. Thomas and Craig Conant, *Citadel to City-State: The Transformation of Greece, 1200–700 B.C.E.* Indianapolis: Indiana University Press, 1999, pp. 11–12.
9. Plutarch, *Life of Theseus*, in *Parallel Lives,* excerpted in *The Rise and Fall of Athens: Nine Greek Lives by Plutarch,* trans. Ian Scott-Kilvert. New York: Penguin, 1960, pp. 25–26.
10. Luce, *Lost Atlantis*, pp. 83–84.
11. Martin, *Ancient Greece*, pp. 31–32.
12. Thomas and Conant, *Citadel to City-State*, pp. 44–45.

## Chapter 2: The Rise of City-States and Greece's Rebirth

13. Victor D. Hanson, *The Other Greeks: The Family Farm and the Agrarian Roots of Western Civilization.* New York: Simon and Schuster, 1995, pp. 31, 35.
14. Polybius, *Histories*, published as *Polybius: The Rise of the Roman Empire,* trans. Ian Scott-Kilvert. New York: Penguin, 1979, p. 509.
15. Freeman, *Greek Achievement*, p. 50.
16. Pomeroy et al., *Ancient Greece*, pp. 79–80.
17. Starr, *Ancient Greeks*, p. 15.

## Chapter 3: Men of Marathon: The First Defeat of Persia

18. Philip de Souza, *The Greek and Persian Wars, 499–386 B.C.* London: Osprey, 2003, p. 12.

19. Quoted in Herodotus, *The Histories*, trans. Aubrey de Sélincourt. New York: Penguin, 1972, p. 359.
20. Herodotus, *Histories*, p. 380.
21. Herodotus, *Histories*, p. 382.
22. Herodotus, *Histories*, p. 395.
23. Peter Green, *The Greco-Persian Wars*. Berkeley: University of California Press, 1996, pp. 36–37.
24. Plutarch, *Life of Themistocles*, in *Rise and Fall of Athens*, pp. 80–81.
25. Herodotus, *Histories*, p. 441.
26. Herodotus, *Histories*, pp. 518–19.
27. Quoted in Plutarch, *Themistocles*, in *Rise and Fall of Athens*, p. 88.
28. Quoted in Herodotus, *Histories*, p. 489.
29. Plutarch, *Themistocles*, in *Rise and Fall of Athens*, p. 92.
30. Aeschylus, *The Persians*, in *Aeschylus: Prometheus Bound, The Suppliants, Seven Against Thebes, The Persians*, trans. Philip Vellacott. Baltimore, MD: Penguin, 1961, pp. 133–34.

# Chapter 4: Imperial Athens: Its Golden Age and Rivalry with Sparta

31. W.G. Hardy, *The Greek and Roman World*. Cambridge, MA: Schenkman, 1962, p. 11.
32. Chester G. Starr, *A History of the Ancient World*. New York: Oxford University Press, 1991, p. 275.
33. Quoted in Thucydides, *The Peloponnesian War*, trans. Rex Warner. New York: Penguin, 1972, p. 148.
34. Thucydides, *Peloponnesian War*, pp. 45–46.
35. Thucydides, *Peloponnesian War*, pp. 75–76.
36. Thucydides, *Peloponnesian War*, p. 93.
37. Freeman, *Greek Achievement*, pp. 192–93.
38. Quoted in Thucydides, *Peloponnesian War*, pp. 147–49.
39. Plutarch, *Life of Pericles*, in *Rise and Fall of Athens*, pp. 177, 179.
40. Thucydides, *Peloponnesian War*, p. 41.
41. Pomeroy et al., *Ancient Greece*, pp. 139–41.
42. Paul Cartledge, *The Spartans: The World of the Warrior-Heroes of Ancient Greece, from Utopia to Crisis and Collapse*. New York: Overlook, 2003, p. 29.
43. Donald Kagan, *The Peloponnesian War*. New York: Viking, 2003, p. xxiv.

# Chapter 5: Macedonia Eclipses the City-States

44. Martin, *Ancient Greece*, pp. 175, 177.
45. Kagan, *Peloponnesian War*, p. xxiv.
46. Isocrates, *Address to Philip*, in George Norlin and Larue Van Hook, trans., *Isocrates*. 3 vols. Cambridge, MA: Harvard University Press, 1928–1954, vol. 1, p. 172.
47. Michael Grant, *The Classical Greeks*. New York: Scribner's, 1989, p. 197.
48. Cartledge, *Spartans*, p. 228.
49. Xenophon, *Hellenica*, published as *A History of My Times*, trans. Rex Warner. New York: Penguin, 1979, p. 403.
50. Peter Green, *Alexander of Macedon, 356–323 B.C.: A Historical Biography*. Berkeley: University of California Press, 1991, p. 6.

51. Victor D. Hanson, *The Wars of the Ancient Greeks and Their Invention of Western Military Culture.* London: Cassell, 1999, p. 150.

52. Demosthenes, *First Philippic,* in *Olynthiacs, Philippics, Minor Speeches,* trans. J.H. Vince. Cambridge, MA: Harvard University Press, 1962, pp. 73–75.

53. Plutarch, *Life of Demosthenes,* in *The Age of Alexander: Nine Greek Lives by Plutarch,* trans. Ian Scott-Kilvert. New York: Penguin, 1973, p. 203.

54. Green, *Alexander of Macedon,* p. 32.

55. Pomeroy et al., *Ancient Greece,* p. 390.

# Chapter 6: Alexander the Great: The Second Defeat of Persia

56. Quoted in Arrian, *Anabasis Alexandri* 5.26, passage trans. Don Nardo.

57. J.F.C. Fuller, *The Generalship of Alexander the Great.* New Brunswick, NJ: Rutgers University Press, 1960, p. 292.

58. Green, *Alexander of Macedon,* p. 151.

59. Hanson, *Wars of the Ancient Greeks,* p. 166.

60. Arrian, *Anabasis Alexandri,* published as *The Campaigns of Alexander,* trans. Aubrey de Sélincourt. New York: Penguin, 1971, pp. 72–74.

61. Arrian, *Anabasis,* pp. 120–21.

62. Quoted in Arrian, *Anabasis,* pp. 126–28.

63. Arrian, *Anabasis,* pp. 143–44.

64. Nicholas Sekunda and John Warry, *Alexander the Great: His Armies and Campaigns, 334–323 B.C.* London: Osprey, 1998, p. 89.

65. Plutarch, *Life of Alexander,* in *Age of Alexander,* pp. 281–82.

66. Plutarch, *Alexander,* in *Age of Alexander,* pp. 290–91.

67. Arrian, *Anabasis,* p. 183.

68. Quoted in Plutarch, *Alexander,* in *Age of Alexander,* p. 300.

69. Plutarch, *Alexander,* in *Age of Alexander,* p. 301.

70. Arrian, *Anabassis,* p. 298.

# Chapter 7: The Successor States and Greece's Decline

71. Demetrius of Phaleron, *On Fortune,* quoted in M.M. Austin, ed., *The Hellenistic World from Alexander to the Roman Conquest: A Selection of Ancient Sources in Translation.* Cambridge, England: Cambridge University Press, 1981, pp. 37–38.

72. Peter Green, *Alexander to Actium: The Historical Evolution of the Hellenistic Age.* Berkeley: University of California Press, 1990, p. 319.

73. Michael Grant, *From Alexander to Cleopatra: The Hellenistic World.* New York: Charles Scribner's Sons, 1982, p. xiii.

74. Graham Shipley, *The Greek World After Alexander, 323–30 B.C.* London: Routledge, 2000, pp. 86, 92.

75. Polybius, *Histories,* p. 513.

76. Livy, *History of Rome from Its Foundation,* Books 31–45 excerpted in *Livy: Rome and the Mediterranean,* trans. Henry Bettenson. New York: Penguin, 1976, pp. 320–21.

77. Livy, *History,* in *Rome and the Mediterranean,* pp. 594–95.

# Chronology

## ca. 3000–ca. 1100

Greece's Bronze Age, during which people use tools and weapons made of bronze.

## ca. 2000

Tribal peoples speaking an early form of Greek begin entering the Greek peninsula from the north and northeast; their descendants, whom scholars refer to as Mycenaeans, spread across mainland Greece.

## ca. 1500–ca. 1400

Mycenaean warlords overthrow another early Aegean people, the Minoans, who have long controlled Crete.

## ca. 1200–ca. 1100

For reasons still unclear, the Mycenaean kingdoms and fortresses suffer widespread destruction and rapidly decline.

## ca.1100–ca. 800

Greece's Dark Age, during which poverty and illiteracy are at first widespread and about which modern scholars know very little.

## ca. 850–ca. 750

The most likely period in which the legendary epic poet Homer lived and composed the *Iliad* and *Odyssey*.

## ca. 800–ca. 500

Greece's Archaic Age, characterized by the rise of city-states, the return of prosperity and literacy, rapid population growth, and intensive colonization of the Mediterranean and Black seas.

## 776

Traditional date for the first Olympic Games, held at Olympia, in the northwestern Peloponnesus.

## 594

The Athenians appoint a leading citizen named Solon archon (administrator), charging him with the task of revising Athens's social and political system.

## ca. 559

Cyrus II, "the Great," founds the Persian Empire (centered in what is now Iran), whose rulers, interests, and conquests will consistently affect Greek history and affairs.

## 508

Building on Solon's reforms, an aristocrat named Cleisthenes and his supporters transform Athens's government into the world's first democracy.

## ca. 500–323

Greece's Classical Age, during which Greek arts, architecture, literature, and democratic reforms reach their height.

## 490

The Persian ruler Darius sends an expedition to sack Athens but the Athenians decisively defeat the invaders at Marathon, northeast of Athens.

### 480

Darius's son, Xerxes, launches a massive invasion of Greece; the Greeks win a series of stunning victories and in the following year expel the Persians from the Aegean sphere.

### 461

A leading democratic politician named Pericles becomes Athens's most influential leader.

### 447

Construction begins on a major new temple complex atop Athens's Acropolis; nine years later, the magnificent Parthenon temple is dedicated to the goddess Athena.

### 431

Sparta declares war on Athens, initiating the disastrous Peloponnesian War, which engulfs and exhausts almost all the city-states.

### 404

Athens surrenders, ending the great war and initiating a Spartan hegemony (domination) of Greece.

### 371

The Theban leader Epaminondas defeats the Spartans at Leuctra (near Thebes) and soon afterward invades the Peloponnesus, initiating a period of Theban hegemony.

### 359

King Philip II takes charge of the disunited, culturally backward kingdom of Macedonia and soon begins to forge Europe's first national standing army.

### 338

Philip and his teenage son, Alexander (who will later be called "the Great"), defeat an alliance of city-states at Chaeronea (in western Boeotia).

### 334–323

After Philip's assassination, Alexander invades Persia, carves out the largest empire the world has yet seen, and dies in the Persian capital of Babylon.

### 323–30

Greece's Hellenistic Age, during which Alexander's generals, the so-called Successors, war among themselves and divide his empire into several new kingdoms, which then proceed to also fight among themselves; during the second half of this period, Rome gains control of the Greek world.

### ca. 280

Three large Greek monarchies (the Macedonian, Seleucid, and Ptolemaic kingdoms) emerge from the chaos of the long wars of the Successors.

### 200–197

Rome prosecutes and wins the Second Macedonian War against Macedonia's King Philip V.

### 171–168

Rome wins the Third Macedonian War against Philip's son, Perseus, and dismantles the Macedonian Kingdom.

### 146

A Roman general destroys the once-great Greek city of Corinth as an object lesson to any Greeks contemplating rebellion against Rome.

**31**

The Roman leader Octavian (the future emperor Augustus) defeats the Roman general Mark Antony and Greek queen of Egypt, Cleopatra, at Actium, in western Greece; the following year, the legendary queen, last of the Hellenistic and major autonomous Greek rulers of antiquity, takes her own life.

# For Further Reading

## Books

Peter Connolly, *The Greek Armies*. Morristown, NJ: Silver Burdette, 1979. A fine, detailed study of Greek armor, weapons, and battle tactics, filled with colorful, accurate illustrations. Highly recommended.

Robert B. Kebric, *Greek People*. Mountain View, CA: Mayfield, 2001. A superb overview of major ancient Greek figures from all walks of life.

Michael Kerrigan, *Ancient Greece and the Mediterranean*. New York: Dorling Kindersley, 2001. This brief but useful overview of ancient Greek civilization, aimed at beginners in the subject, is filled with stunning color photos of locales and artifacts.

Don Nardo, *Greek Temples*. New York: Franklin Watts, 2002. A colorfully illustrated overview of how Greek temples were built and used. Written for younger readers.

———, *Greenhaven Encyclopedia of Greek and Roman Mythology*. San Diego: Greenhaven Press, 2002. Contains hundreds of short but informative articles on Greek myths, gods, heroes, and the myth tellers and their works.

———, *Women of Ancient Greece*. San Diego: Lucent Books, 2000. A detailed look at all aspects of the lives of women in the ancient Greek city-states.

## Internet Sources

Hellenic Museum and Cultural Center, "A Day in the Life of an Ancient Greek." www.hellenicmuseum.org/exhibits/dayinlife.html. A useful, easy-to-read general source for ancient Greek life, including clothes, food, sports, art, and more.

PBS, "The Greeks: Crucible of Civilization." www.pbs.org/empires/thegreeks. Excellent online resource based on the acclaimed PBS show. Has numerous links to sites containing information about ancient Greek history and culture.

Tufts University Department of the Classics, "Perseus Project." www.perseus.tufts.edu. The most comprehensive online source about ancient Greece, with hundreds of links to all aspects of Greek history, life, and culture, supported by numerous photos of artifacts.

# Works Consulted

## Major Works

Paul Cartledge, *The Spartans: The World of the Warrior-Heroes of Ancient Greece, from Utopia to Crisis and Collapse.* New York: Overlook, 2003. A masterful overview of Sparta and its relations with other Greek states by the leading scholar of ancient Sparta.

Rodney Castleden, *Minoans: Life in Bronze Age Crete.* New York: Routledge, 1993. A good general synopsis of the Minoans.

Robert Drews, *The Coming of the Greeks: Indo-European Conquests in the Aegean and the Near East.* Princeton, NJ: Princeton University Press, 1988. Discusses the prevailing theories for the settling of mainland Greece and nearby islands before and during the Bronze Age.

J.R. Ellis, *Philip II and Macedonian Imperialism.* New York: Thames and Hudson, 1977. One of the best modern studies of the rise of Philip and Macedonia.

Charles Freeman, *The Greek Achievement: The Foundation of the Western World.* New York: Viking, 1999. A well-written overview of ancient Greek civilization, touching on cultural endeavors as well as history.

Michael Grant, *The Rise of the Greeks.* New York: Macmillan, 1987. A superb examination of the rise of city-states in Greece, with detailed studies of nearly fifty separate states.

Peter Green, *Alexander of Macedon, 356–323 B.C.: A Historical Biography.* Berkeley: University of California Press, 1991. One of the two or three best available overviews of Alexander and his exploits, by one of the leading classical historians of the past century.

———, *Alexander to Actium: The Historical Evolution of the Hellenistic Age.* Berkeley: University of California Press, 1990. This huge tome is the most comprehensive study of Greece's Hellenistic Age written to date.

———, *The Greco-Persian Wars.* Berkeley: University of California Press, 1996. An excellent overview of the Greek repulse of Persia from 490 to 479 B.C.

Victor D. Hanson, *The Wars of the Ancient Greeks and Their Invention of Western Military Culture.* London: Cassell, 1999. A fine general study of ancient Greek military methods, battles, and wars.

Donald Kagan, *The Peloponnesian War.* New York: Viking, 2003. A renowned scholar masterfully summarizes the long and devastating conflict that involved nearly all of the Greek city-states.

Thomas R. Martin, *Ancient Greece: From Prehistoric to Hellenistic Times.* New Haven, CT: Yale University Press, 1996.

One of the best general overviews of Greek history and culture on the market.

Sarah B. Pomeroy et al., *Ancient Greece: A Political, Social, and Cultural History.* New York: Oxford University Press, 1999. A very well-organized, detailed, and insightful summary of ancient Greek civilization.

Graham Shipley, *The Greek World After Alexander, 323–30 B.C.* London: Routledge, 2000. A superior overview of the Hellenistic Age, successor states, and the decline of Greece.

Carol G. Thomas and Craig Conant, *Citadel to City-State: The Transformation of Greece, 1200–700 B.C.E.* Indianapolis: Indiana University Press, 1999. This examination of Greece in the Dark and Archaic ages is well written and worthwhile.

# Other Important Works
## Primary Sources

Aeschylus, *Aeschylus: Prometheus Bound, The Suppliants, Seven Against Thebes, The Persians.* Trans. Philip Vellacott. Baltimore, MD: Penguin, 1961.

Arrian, *Anabasis Alexandri*, published as *The Campaigns of Alexander.* Trans. Aubrey de Sélincourt. New York: Penguin, 1971.

M.M. Austin, ed., *The Hellenistic World from Alexander to the Roman Conquest: A Selection of Ancient Sources in Translation.* Cambridge, England: Cambridge University Press, 1981.

Demosthenes, *Olynthiacs, Philippics, Minor Speeches.* Trans. J.H. Vince. Cambridge, MA: Harvard University Press, 1962.

Diodorus Siculus, *Library of History.* Various trans. 12 vols. Cambridge, MA: Harvard University Press, 1962–1967.

Herodotus, *The Histories.* Trans. Aubrey de Sélincourt. New York: Penguin, 1972.

Homer, *Iliad.* Trans. E.V. Rieu. Baltimore, MD: Penguin, 1950.

———, *Odyssey.* Trans. E.V. Rieu. Baltimore, MD: Penguin, 1961.

Isocrates, surviving works in George Norlin and Larue Van Hook, trans., *Isocrates.* 3 vols. Cambridge, MA: Harvard University Press, 1928–1954.

Livy, *History of Rome from Its Foundation,* Books 31–45 excerpted in *Livy: Rome and the Mediterranean.* Trans. Henry Bettenson. New York: Penguin, 1976.

Plutarch, *Parallel Lives,* excerpted in *The Rise and Fall of Athens: Nine Greek Lives by Plutarch.* Trans. Ian Scott-Kilvert. New York: Penguin, 1960; also excerpted in *The Age of Alexander: Nine Greek Lives by Plutarch.* Trans. Ian Scott-Kilvert. New York: Penguin, 1973.

Polybius, *Histories,* published as *Polybius: The Rise of the Roman Empire.* Trans. Ian Scott-Kilvert. New York: Penguin, 1979.

Thucydides, *The Peloponnesian War.* Trans. Rex Warner. New York: Penguin, 1972.

Xenophon, *Hellenica,* published as *A History of My Times.* Trans. Rex Warner. New York: Penguin, 1979.

## Modern Sources

Lesly Adkins and Roy A. Adkins, *Handbook to Life in Ancient Greece.* New York: Facts On File, 1997.

Peter Connolly, *Greece and Rome at War.* London: Greenhill Books, 1998.

J.K. Davies, *Democracy and Classical Greece*. Cambridge, MA: Harvard University Press, 1993.

Robert Drews, *The End of the Bronze Age: Changes in Warfare and the Catastrophe ca. 1200 B.C.* Princeton, NJ: Princeton University Press, 1993.

Will Durant, *The Life of Greece*. New York: Simon and Schuster, 1966.

J. Lesley Fitton, *Discovery of the Greek Bronze Age*. London: British Museum Press, 1995.

J.F.C. Fuller, *The Generalship of Alexander the Great*. New Brunswick, NJ: Rutgers University Press, 1960.

Michael Grant, *The Classical Greeks*. New York: Scribner's, 1989.

———, *From Alexander to Cleopatra: The Hellenistic World*. New York: Charles Scribner's Sons, 1982.

N.G.L. Hammond, *A History of Greece to 322 B.C.* Oxford, England: Clarendon Press, 1986.

———, *Philip of Macedon*. Baltimore, MD: Johns Hopkins University Press, 1994.

Victor D. Hanson, *The Other Greeks: The Family Farm and the Agrarian Roots of Western Civilization*. New York: Simon and Schuster, 1995.

———, *The Western Way of War: Infantry Battle in Classical Greece*. New York: Oxford University Press, 1989.

W.G. Hardy, *The Greek and Roman World*. Cambridge, MA: Schenkman, 1962.

Donald Kagan, *Pericles of Athens and the Birth of Democracy*. New York: Free Press, 1991.

J.V. Luce, *Lost Atlantis: New Light on an Old Legend*. New York: McGraw-Hill, 1969.

Christian Meier, *Athens: Portrait of a City in Its Golden Age*. Trans. Robert and Rita Kimber. New York: Henry Holt, 1998.

A.J. Podlecki, *The Life of Themistocles*. Montreal, Canada: McGill-Queen's University Press, 1975.

Nicholas Sekunda, *Marathon, 490 B.C.: The First Persian Invasion of Greece*. Oxford, England: Osprey, 2002.

Nicholas Sekunda and John Warry, *Alexander the Great: His Armies and Campaigns, 334–323 B.C.* London: Osprey, 1998.

A.M. Snodgrass, *Archaic Greece*. Berkeley: University of California Press, 1980.

Philip de Souza, *The Greek and Persian Wars, 499–386 B.C.* London: Osprey, 2003.

Chester G. Starr, *The Ancient Greeks*. New York: Oxford University Press, 1971.

———, *A History of the Ancient World*. New York: Oxford University Press, 1991.

———, *The Origins of Greek Civilization, 1100–650 B.C.* New York: Knopf, 1961.

William Taylour, *The Mycenaeans*. London: Thames and Hudson, 1983.

George D. Wilcoxon, *Athens Ascendant*. Ames: Iowa State University Press, 1979.

# Index

# Picture Credits

Cover: © Premium Stock/CORBIS
The Art Archive/Archaeological
   Museum/Florence/Dagli Orti ,16
© Araldo de Luca/CORBIS ,38, 73
© Bettmann/CORBIS, 7, 19, 26, 29,
   45, 46, 49, 55, 74, 78, 79, 87
© Gianni Dagli Orti/CORBIS, 61
© North Carolina Museum of
   Art/CORBIS, 77
© Sandro Vannini/CORBIS, 95
© Ruggero Varro/CORBIS, 88

© Vanni Archive/CORBIS, 66
Hulton Archive/Getty Images, 13, 34
Joseph Paris Picture Archive, 42, 58, 70
Chris Jouan, 26, 75, 85
Mary Evans Picture Library, 15, 18, 34,
   36, 56, 67
North Wind Picture Archives, 9, 28, 43,
   53, 62, 69, 81
Peck's Pictorial, 33
Courtesy of Richmond University, 71
Steve Zmina, 12, 21, 31, 65, 94

# About the Author

Historian Don Nardo has written or edited numerous volumes about the ancient Greek world, including *Greek and Roman Sport, The Age of Pericles, The Parthenon, Life in Ancient Athens, The Decline and Fall of Ancient Greece,* and literary companions to the works of Homer, Euripides, and Sophocles. He resides with his wife, Christine, in Massachusetts.